FRIENDS DIVIDED

CONFLICT AND DIVISION IN THE SOCIETY OF FRIENDS

BY

DAVID E. W. HOLDEN

Friends United Press
Richmond, Indiana

LIBRARY OF CONGRESS
Library of Congress Cataloging-in-Publication Data

Holden, David E. W.
    Friends divided : conflict and division in the Society of Friends
/ by David E.W. Holden.
        p.   cm.
    Bibliography: p.
    Includes index.
    ISBN 0-944350-06-2
    1. Society of Friends — History.   I. Title
BX7631.2.H64 1988
289.6'09 — dc19

This is lovingly dedicated to the memory of my parents, Edward Holden and Marian Barker Holden of Mexico City. Both are greatly missed.

Table of Contents

ACKNOWLEDGMENTS

This book began with a simple question: "What makes a member of the Society of Friends?" In trying to find an answer that would not lead to conflict, I went into the history of the Society and found that the question had a number of answers, not one of which satisfied everyone. I also found that Friends used to deprive each other of membership and that the Society of Friends has divided into several different branches, each of which dealt with membership in its own way.

Intrigued by what appeared to be a violation of the testimony Friends have of not proceeding until they have reached unity, I read further. My questions now broadened to include: "How could Friends, with their theology of continual revelation based on the availability of immediate contact with the Divine that was open to all, divide into permanent factions?" And: "How could a group of people so wedded to the ideas of peace and reconciliation divide so acrimoniously that they denied the validity of each other's beliefs only a few years later?" I hoped that asking these questions would help Friends avoid future conflict.

Ten years later I am not at all certain I can help Friends overcome their divisions. The differences that exist between them are too great for that. Perhaps an understanding of these differences will allow them to accept each other as Quakers. All the branches share the same roots; all have grown and developed in their own ways, and all are valid for the people who are in them. They differ socially, ideologically and theologically, but they all provide meaning for their own.

I have been helped to complete this book by many people. On two occasions Queen's University has given me sabbatical leave for the project. The first leave was spent at Woodbrooke College in Selly Oak, Birmingham, England, where I was the Woodbrooke Fellow for the year in 1975-6. The second came six years later. It was spent at the Earlham School of Religion as their scholar in residence. The first period allowed me to expose my ignorance and begin the work. At Earlham I was able to do the bulk of the writing that eventually led to this book. Financial help was provided by: Canada Council in the form of a leave fellowship in 1975-6; Woodbrooke College also in the form of fellowship; a leave grant from Queen's University; and, a grant from Earlham School of Religion. To all of these I express my profound thanks.

I have been given advice, information and encouragement by many people at different stages of the work. Among the most helpful were Maurice Creasey, Hugh Barbour, Wilmer Cooper, Harold Tollefson, Algie Newlin and Phillip C. Shore. At Earlham the people in Lilly Library were extremely helpful. They pulled things out of the archives, found books for me and gave me space to work. They went the second and even the third mile in acquiring material that I needed for the work. Each of these people has helped to make my work easier and to improve the quality of the material I produced. I could not have done it without them. Also, I have been allowed open access to records, libraries, and archives in: Haverford College, Swarthmore College, Friends University, Guilford College, Friends United Meeting, Western Yearly Meeting, Central Yearly Meeting, Canadian Yearly Meeting, Pickering College and, of course, Lilly Library and Woodbrooke College. My thanks go to all of them. I should also mention my thanks to Margaret Springer who provided me with the title for this book. I can not leave out one person who has contributed immensely to the quality of this book. My thanks goes to my editor, Barbara Mays, without whom this book would not have been completed.

Finally, there is one person who has helped me more than anyone else, a person who did more than all the others to make this possible. She encouraged, challenged, helped, criticized, cajoled, supported and gave me the will to finish. She has kept me honest and has done a great deal to give me the understanding that made the whole section on the Midwest possible. Without her help I would never have managed to do what was done. She began by challenging some of the strange ideas I had of Midwestern pastoral Friends. She then showed me some of the variety that exists there. She arranged for interviews and visits that without her services as a "native informant" I could never have managed. Through her I was able to gather the material on Central Yearly Meeting. It was there that I discovered just how different Friends can really be, as I simply did not understand the meaning of their religious language. This person is my wife, Joyce Mardock Holden. She helped enormously but is not to be held responsible for the faults in this work. They are my own.

Introduction

The Peace Testimony is one of Friends oldest testimonies. Friends have tried particularly hard and have suffered greatly in the cause of peace. It is surprising, therefore, that conflict is central to the origin of the Society, its early growth and its subsequent development. Friends history of disagreement, withdrawal, disownment for sacrilege, heresy, and schism begins before the Society of Friends acquired its name. The potential for conflict has always been there and is present today. The accounts that follow are intended to provide an understanding of them in their historical context. Friends peculiarities, their "ways," are a product of their experience. Much of their character has come as a result of conflict.

When Friends write about themselves they write about the things that inspire them. Their history tends to glorify earlier people and events. They concentrate on acts of heroism and virtue. Martyrdom suffered joyously, success against enormous odds, idealism in the face of the "enemy" (whoever he, or she, may be) are what people want to read. The nasty things like conflict and division are neglected. Once in awhile a disagreement becomes so important it simply cannot be ignored. When this happens the disagreement is described but the author may do it to make a point about the "wickedness" of those who have separated or been disowned. Only a few histories have dealt with internal conflict in detail.

Furthermore, most religious histories limit themselves to the strictly religious events, and Quakers are no exception. It is as if the only information suitable for a Friends history is what takes place in meetings and is recorded in the minutes. Material that is found in diaries, letters between Friends, and in their journals is also included. The ordinary things and events that "everyone knows about" are not described. The result for those of us who come later is that we miss the anecdotes, and history is dull.

1

The knowledge most Friends have of their early history is limited to the history as found in George Fox's Journal[1], which is modified for some by his letter to the Governor of Barbadoes[2]. The Journal, however, was meant to be an account of Fox's spiritual journey and was written after the events he describes. The letter to the Governor of Barbadoes, written in 1671, is an orthodox statement of belief that was written at a time of stress, when Friends were being persecuted and imprisoned. It was written to make their treatment easier. Only later did it become one of the central statements of belief at another time when the Society of Friends was experiencing a great deal of conflict and change — see the chapters below on the period after the American Civil War.

People are central to what takes place in history. They act according to their inspiration, foibles and their strong likes and dislikes. When people act in groups they act according to their culture and the context they face. The culture and the social context provide the basic list of choices people have when they choose to act. Here the term culture is used in the anthropological sense meaning the norms, social structure and, in fact, everything a person learns as a member of a society. One can only preach, for example, when: a) there is someone to preach to; b) there is something to preach about; c) there is a time and place that allow it; and d) when there are enough ideas and values shared by the preacher and audience to make the message meaningful. It is all of this and more that allows social events to take place.

The context for the beginning of the Society of Friends was in the period of turmoil after a revolution in England at the end of the Medieval period and after the Protestant Reformation was well underway. The earliest Friends were mainly farmers. In a very short time, however, they moved into urban life. In America, Friends were first divided between urban and rural groups. Later with the move west they were also divided between the frontier and the eastern seaboard. Each group of Friends reinterpreted their theology in light of their own experience. The changes produced left English Friends more like the urban Friends of the Eastern seaboard than the others.

An important part of understanding conflict in the Society of Friends is to understand the role of new ideas. Although a few Friends have tried to live in isolation, the majority worked out their lives in the world, often trying to reform it. Being a part of the world has meant being open to new ideas from that world. The turmoil of the world's ideas has continually made Friends reinterpret the Light they are given. In the process, new ideas have become a part of Friends thinking.

New ideas can be troublesome when they challenge old and dearly respected ideas or practices. The introduction of prayer meetings and hymns in the American Midwest in the nineteenth century is a case in point. Just as troublesome are old ideas given new emphasis, as was the renewed emphasis on the Bible at the end of the eighteenth century. New ideas are troublesome not because they make people think in new ways but because they frequently lead people to change their behavior. Particularly troublesome is that new ideas and their associated practices are not taken up at the same time by everyone.

When bonds of family and friendship are close, adjustments to new ideas can easily be made. People can discuss the ideas and come to an agreement on them with relative ease. However, when social bonds are loose, new ideas are not easily shared. Agreement then becomes more difficult. Problems that surface can become important if they involve an important practice. A rediscovered old idea has problems, too, because the social context has changed. For example, the rediscovery of the Bible by Friends in the late eighteenth and early nineteenth century was not the same as their original discovery. In the seventeenth century it was the first and only book they had to read. They learned reading just to read the Bible. In the nineteenth century the Bible's return to importance was in a very changed context. Reading was something many could do and there were many books that could be read. Reading the Bible became a matter of religious importance, something that had been neglected for a long time. An aspect of the changed context was that later questions were raised about the validity and inerrancy of the story in relation to received inspiration. Such questions were not part of the context of the earlier period.

Friends have examined and argued about ideas for much of their history. This is one of the reasons given for their gatherings. When a new idea is introduced it is usually espoused by a single person or a small group. People with new ideas can be "dealt with" if the idea is potentially harmful. However, persuasive ideas, even harmful ones, often do not go away. When new ideas reappear and are held by a larger group, "dealing" is often much more difficult. The group which is "dealt with" may turn out to be stronger than expected.

When new ideas combine with unresolved problems divisions may come about. A single new idea is quite unlikely to cause a division. The combination of heretical ideas with other strong ideas, a refusal to listen, and time causes division. Division comes only after the two sides have stewed in their disagreement for years and have quit

3

talking to each other. A further requirement is that people take sides on all issues uniformly, so that the division is clear. If they do not do so then a great deal of heat may be generated, along with anger and hurt feelings, but the division will be avoided.

This book is about conflict and division in the Religious Society of Friends, something most Friends find hard. Perhaps by examining something hard, future damage can be avoided. I should add, at the outset, that with today's differences a united Religious Society of Friends will remain a dream.

The Beginning

1

The Early Days and First Troubles

The Seekers of 1652 lived in the dales of northern England. Their customs grew out of their experience of trying to survive farming the poor soils of the dales. They worried about getting enough to pay for basic necessities and to cover the cost of rent, tithes and taxes. They had also found ways to defend themselves against their landlords and the earlier raids from the Scots and the North Sea pirates.

To produce as much as they could from their small, poor, farms everybody, with their animals, was expected to move to the hilltops in the Spring. Then the good land could be used undisturbed to grow as much as possible. Annual movement of this kind required unanimity. The practice of finding a "sense of the meeting" was, therefore, in place long before Fox appeared. Their agreement to move was based on custom, but the time they chose to move was decided at a meeting of the villagers.[1]

This mechanism of arriving at a consensus is not unique to the Seekers. It has been used as an argument for the virtue of Indian tribes in Canada by recently acculturated members of those tribes. In my work on the Cree in northern Quebec, this aspect of their decision making process is obvious. Lewis Benson contended that Fox's "Gospel Order" as applied to the structure he imposed on Friends[2] was given by God, and it may well have been so. However, God gave the gift to others as well, among them were the Cree and people of the dales. Fox had observed it in action there and made it a central practice of Friends.

In the villages of the dales, a single person who refused to agree could cause a lot of harm. The community enforced its agreement by threat of removal from the community. They removed people simply by taking the offender's house apart. This was not hard to do as houses were made of stone.

Like the rural poor everywhere, the Seekers survived quite nicely when things went well — when the grain was plentiful, the animals were healthy and the pastures thick on the hilltops. In the 1640s crops failed and winters were colder than usual. It added to their burden of forced tithing. To make matters even worse, Parliament and King Charles I had a falling out over power, taxes and the place of the church.

The Civil War in England began with Scotland's refusal to use the English Prayer Book. It became more serious when Parliament refused to pay for the war with the Scots. War finally came when the King retaliated against Parliament. He dismissed Parliament and arrested some of its prominent opposition members. The English Civil War began in 1641 and ended in January, 1649. War with Ireland carried on afterward. That war was no sooner ended than England went to war with Holland. Just after peace was made with Holland, there was a small uprising of Royalists; after it was put down, war with Spain became important. Wars and the threat of uprising kept Cromwell occupied to the end of his life in 1659.

The turmoil of almost constant war, much of it over religion, deprived the farmers of the little support they had from the church. It took their young men away for years at a time.The years allowed the people to discover they could live without the priests. People were found who could do the work of priests yet did not demand the payment of tithes[3]. It left many people with questions about the church, as tithes had been collected regularly. Tithes, never popular, now produced great opposition. Many came to believe that it was wrong to pay tithes in return for nothing.

Another important change in religious life was the introduction of inexpensive Bibles. The Bible was the first inexpensive book available to people in England. For many people it was the only book available.[4] People learned to read so they could study the Scriptures. It was widely read and discussed, and by the middle of the seventeenth century it was probably known in detail by most literate adults.

With no trained priests to lead them in worship, the northerners used their traditional technique: they sat together to decide what to do. At times, while sitting to make community decisions, they centered their meetings on worship. Not knowing what else to do, they would read parts of the Bible and probe its meaning. Silent pauses gave time to mull over the ideas. In this process of seeking, they made many of the ideas their own. When Fox arrived the Seekers already had settled meetings for worship that involved Bible study and waiting in silence. These practices and that of not proceeding until unity was reached became central to the nature of Quakerism.

On a summer's day in 1652 George Fox came to the dales of northern England. He had traveled from the Midlands through Nottinghamshire and Yorkshire, preaching and making converts. He echoed people's thoughts more clearly than anyone had done before. He convinced Richard Farnsworth, James Nayler, William Dewsbury, and many more people who were to play important roles in the Quaker movement. With Fox's inspiration and their own experience, William Dewsbury and Farnsworth established general meetings throughout the North on the Seeker's pattern. Farnsworth's instructions on the matter were quite explicit. Friends were to:

> See that you be there and observe order, and let not the earth hinder or keep back, but keep to the pure that it may guide you and lead you on in the true diligence and obedience.[5]

They created, in effect, a series of cell groups that would continue to mobilize people for a mission to transform England and the world. It was just when George Fox was beginning to travel that these ideas were at their strongest. Christopher Hill wrote:

> From, say, 1645 to 1653 there was a great overturning, questioning, revaluing, of everything in England. Old institutions, old beliefs, old values came into question. Men moved easily from one critical group to another, and a Quaker of the early 1650's had far more in common with a Leveler or a Digger or a Ranter than with a modern member of the Society of Friends.[6]

It was in the period of Fox's early travels that the Levelers became an independent political force with demands for political power. These radicals demanded the abolition of tithes, as well as the removal of honours from the losing Cavaliers.[7] In these two things Friends were but a part of the whole. According to H. N. Brailsford early Friends were in some cases:

> ...frustrated Levelers, defeated in the political realm who had taken to novel ways of carrying on the class struggle, primarily

They were part of the "shattered Baptists" Fox felt were waiting for him everywhere.[9]

George Fox's arrival on Firbank Fell in 1652 was the beginning of the movement that became the Society of Friends. He had traveled and preached for years. However, this was the first time he had found a large and supportive group of people. He made contact with people who were to become very important in the development of Quakerism. Among them was Margaret Fell, the woman who did so much for the Society of Friends that she came to be called the "Mother of Quakerism." The Kendal Fund, which financed the efforts of the traveling ministers, was organized and supervised largely by her efforts. It allowed Margaret Fell to have an important part in introducing the idea of the ministry of women very early in Friends history.

The new movement grew as more became convinced and began to travel in the ministry. It was a phenomenally rapid growth. Early Friends wrote tracts, disputed priests and suffered for their actions. People were ready for the new message, and Friends felt it was important enough to preach to the world. Nayler, Dewsbury, Farnsworth, and Fox began their mission in the midst of turmoil.

Puritans and Presbyterians were fighting for power. Baptists and other "Sectarians" were united against Royalists, Catholics and Common Prayer Men. Sectarians, the new religious groups too small to bother with as individual groups but a large sum in total, filled the nooks and crannies of the body politic. The sheer volume of opposition threatened the people in power. At first, the Quakers were only one of the many sects and were not seen as a threat to anyone. Many early Friends were ex-army men. Some had been part of other sectarian groups, such as Diggers and Levellers.[10]

All these groups had a vision of what life could be. Although they disagreed on the details, all wanted a religious transformation of the world, and this desire had prolonged the English Civil War. Cromwell's eventual victory did not stop the struggle. To pacify a country that had gone through a civil war, things were done that were later regretted. Among them was the execution of Charles I. This was the first regicide in Europe, and it deeply shocked everyone. However, for the religious reformers it was an opening for the return of Christ to rule the world. Why kill a king for any other reason?

The regicide was seen as a positive step for one group. This group, the Fifth Monarchy Men, was so disappointed when Charles II was restored to the throne in 1660 that they rebelled. It was a last desperate attempt to make Christ's rule on earth possible. However, between the time Cromwell obtained control of England and the time Charles II was restored to the throne there was a great deal of trouble, trouble that affected the way the Society of Friends was to develop.

Amidst the turmoil, the Quakers worked to get others to share in their vision. William Dewsbury stated the vision with power:

Now is the Lord appearing in this day of his mighty power, to gather his elect

> together...and is making up his mighty host, and exalting Jesus Christ...to lead his Army he had raised up in the North of England; and is marched towards the South, in the mighty power of the living word, which is sharp as a two edged sword, to cut down the high and low, rich and poor, priest and people...[11]

The inspiration was contagious. It spread quickly throughout England, Wales and Ireland and across the ocean into New England.

In a short time Friends became the largest and, therefore, the most feared sectarian group. The population of England and Wales in 1603 was about 4 million and by 1688 had grown to about 5-1/2 million. The figures for Friends, which are highly suspect, for the same period grew from roughly 30,000 in 1660 to 60,000 in 1680.[12] What makes estimating the number of Friends so difficult is that nobody then tried counting them or tried keeping complete lists of adherents. Membership definition was still a long time into the future.

To the magistrates, Quakers were both dangerous and suspect; their attitude equaled our distrust of cults today. The rude egalitarian ways of Quakers were frightfully annoying. Friends refused to take their hats off to their betters. They used "thee" and "thou," terms then only used toward social inferiors, close friends and relatives, in a most unbecoming way. Some Quaker practices looked like those of another troublesome group, the Ranters.

The Ranters were troublesome for early Friends because the two groups resembled each other superficially. Ranters were people who were convinced that they had received direct inspiration from God. They felt they could do nothing wrong in the eyes of God, even when they harmed others. Non-Ranters found them to be extremely unpleasant to have around. Friends were like Ranters in their belief direct inspiration from God.[13] Further, many Quakers had once been Diggers or Levellers, two groups that were so dangerous they had

11

been put down by force. Because of their numbers, their radical message and their former contacts, the magistrates feared Friends would engage in some form of insurrection. Consequently, the magistrates did all they could to repress Friends, using the laws given them to control groups dangerous to society.

A few of the laws most used at this time to control Friends were the Statutes of Provisors and Praemunire, originally enacted in the reign of Richard II some three centuries earlier to control French influence over the Pope when the Pope lived in Avignon. These required an oath of loyalty to the Crown. Also used were the Elizabethan acts against Puritans which made it a crime to refuse to go to church. It was also a crime to attend assemblies, conventicles or meetings or any such exercise of religion not part of the established church. These were re-enforced by the Clarendon Code after 1662. Blasphemy and refusal to pay tithes were crimes that could be tried in civil or ecclesiatical courts. Blasphemy was potentially a capital crime.

Friends defended themselves and attacked their attackers. They continued to write, preach and debate. They made enemies of Puritans, Baptists, Presbyterians and Episcopalians. They described their sufferings and exhorted their rulers. Often they wrote and printed tracts to deliver their, at times unclear, message.

The biggest bulk of Friends writing was composed of debates with Puritans and others on the subject of religion. Second in frequency in the early years were descriptions of their sufferings, sometimes combined with appeals for the sufferers. Later, when the rate of imprisonment became very high, exhortations and appeals to political leaders dominated. Printed testimonies and epistles were Friends earliest forms of publication and remained popular. The focus of most publications was outward rather than to the converted. In overall numbers, the peak years were 1659-1663. There was a secondary peak in 1675-1680 after which came a second period of severe repression and an exodus to America.[14]

To protect themselves and look after those who were in jail because of the persecution a fund was set up in 1654 at Kendal to be supervised by George Taylor and Thomas Willan "...for the service of the Truth." so "...that there may be some money in stock for disbursing ...either to Friends that go forth into the service or to prisoners necessities..."[15]

The fund grew with regular accounts being sent to Margaret Fell. It was first used to look after the needs of traveling Friends and Friends in prison. Books were also bought with the money. Although Friends refused to pay tithes, they welcomed free contributions for the fund and for the support of Friends in the ministry. By 1659 Hubberthorn felt moved to write:

> Let every one that will preach the gospel live of the gospel, and not upon any settled or state maintenance ... for the cry of honest and godly people of this nation is to have a free ministry and free maintenance, and are willing freely to maintain those that minister unto them the word and doctrine.[16]

Traveling ministers, referred to now as the First Publishers of the Truth, often took the initiative in establishing new meetings. As they could not always stay in one place, they found local people to be elders to "...look after the poor and to see that all walked according to the Truth..."[17] By 1654 their work had created two kinds of meetings: district general meetings and select monthly meetings. The meetings secured the ongoing religious fellowship, provided religious leadership, ministered to the people and attempted to control extreme behavior.[18] Select meetings were for the elders who were given special responsibilities. General meetings were gatherings for all to worship publicly together.

Friends spread south. By 1654 they were working in Bristol and London and had spread to Ireland. In 1655 there were enough Friends in London to buy the Bull and Mouth Tavern, a building large enough to hold a thousand people.[19] With success came increased persecution. Quakers were harassed, assaulted, and a lot of anti-Quaker material was published. The charges, countercharges and general disturbance were enough to get the central government to constrain Friends from "irregular and disorderly practices."[20]

Rapid growth, and persecution, set the stage for the first major internal confrontation. In June, 1655, James Nayler, then one of the best known Friends, traveled to London. He had been imprisoned at Appleby for heresy, for having said "thou" to a magistrate and for refusing to remove his hat. He had also tried to mediate the conflict with Rice Jones, the leader of the first split in the new movement.[21]

In London, Nayler was spectacularly successful. By 1656 he had become the chief spokesman and had attracted a strong personal following. His prominence made him the focus of attacks on the Quakers. Some members were so strongly in his favor they resented the work done by other Quaker ministers. Nayler's supporters disrupted the meetings organized by other Friends, something Friends were not supposed to do to each other. They felt all Friends, including George Fox, should submit to Nayler.[22]

The disruption was reported to Fox, then in the Launceston Prison. Nayler, in an attempt to make amends, traveled to see Fox, but on his way he was jailed in Exeter. Two of Nayler's supporters, Martha Simmonds and Hannah Stranger, traveled by Launceston to get Fox to submit to Nayler. On his release, Fox stopped at Exeter to visit Nayler in prison. There the two quarreled and parted. Each felt that the other was profoundly wrong and had not behaved acceptably.[23]

When Nayler was released, he traveled to Bristol, and arrived on October 24, 1656 with Stranger and Simmonds. The two women led Nayler's horse into town singing "Holy, holy, holy, Lord King of Israel." They spread their cloaks in front of him and knelt down to him. They had arrived in the pouring rain, so the party of seven people was seen by almost nobody. Friends had stayed away in protest.[24] However, Nayler and his party were seen by the police, who arrested him and charged him with blasphemy.

The Bristol magistrates who arrested Nayler were friends of a Puritan priest that had lost many of his flock to the Quakers. The chance to get revenge, to suppress Quakers, to rid the world of a blasphemer, and to get at Cromwell all at the same time was too hard to resist. James Nayler was sent down to London to face Parliament and answer to the charge incurred by

> ...the damnable and blasphemous doctrines of the Quakers which tend in their own nature to the utter ruin of the true Christian religion and civil government...[25].

Actions like Nayler's had previously been dealt with locally, but new political conditions changed matters. Nayler's case was ideal to use to embarrass Cromwell. Earlier, Cromwell had been forced to call an election to get a Parliament that would provide the revenue needed to run the country. He had chosen his candidates carefully and had arranged it all to his satisfaction. That attempt failed, and Cromwell was forced to call another election. At this time the people who had been excluded wanted to embarrass him, and Nayler's case came forward at just the right time.

After several days of debate in Parliament, much of it procedural in nature, James Nayler was found guilty and sentenced. His punishment was to sit two hours in the pillory in Westminster, then be whipped through the streets to the Old Exchange in London — a distance of about two and a half miles — and sit two hours in that pillory. He was branded on the forehead and had his tongue bored

14

through with a red hot iron. Finally, he was imprisoned in isolation to work for his sustenance. There was a tremendous outcry over the brutality of the sentence. In time Nayler was released. He died about a year later after a reconciliation with Fox.[26]

Nayler, in Geoffrey Nuttal's words had and "...attitude of utter, immediate dependence upon God, without the recognition of any human medium or instrumentality..."[27] It led him to allow his followers to act as they did in Bristol. To Fox it was obvious that Nayler's isolation from the judgment of others in the Friends community was dangerous to the new movement. Between 1652 and 1656 Fox had begun to understand the need to check the extremes of religiously based behavior, extremes that were obvious in the Ranters. It was this need that had served as the basis for his disagreement with Nayler. After Nayler's trial more severe persecution submerged the shock and notoriety from the trial. Friends now began to have a greater appreciation of the value of regularly held general and select meetings.

2
Consolidating and Controlling the Change

During the five years of persecution which lead up to the Restoration in 1660, Friends began to consolidate their gains. They dealt with dissidents and worked to make their movement grow. The disputes with non-Friends continued, which only made persecution harsher. Persecution drew people into the movement instead of driving them away. In spite of the persecution and the growth in numbers, Friends began to pay attention to the internal needs of their movement. General meetings became more common, and some Friends traveled to North America.

By the end of the Protectorate, the sporadic and *ad hoc* arrangements for holding Friends general meetings were becoming more permanent. Even when persecution was at its peak, Friends met regularly to care for the poor, visit the sick, and find work for those who lost it in cause of the Truth. This work began in London in 1656.[1]

When the unparalleled persecution began in 1660, Friends had only the idea of a possible organization: the one they had used to resist the depredations of northern landlords. Their leadership was composed of self-selected Publishers of the Truth, who had an informal support system and a small fund. They also had small and scattered groups of people like those who had taken part in the "General Meeting of Friends in the Truth" held at Balby and the one held in Hampshire in 1659. These were people who had either experienced persecution or had been "converted." They had written letters to Friends on the conduct of worship and their lives, collected

16

funds, and reviewed the work done by other meetings. They acted rather like Friends yearly meeting committees do today. Collecting reports of sufferings had become a very important activity the select meetings did in the "service of the truth."

The meeting of Elders at Balby in Yorkshire was held in November, 1656. They set out a list of advices that Braithwaite saw as the joint conclusion of the whole meeting. The items include: times at which meetings should be held; organization of new meetings; dealing with those ceasing to attend meeting for worship or "who walk disorderly." The Elders kept records on births, marriages and deaths and on marital and family behavior, public service and the payment of debts. At the end, in a postscript signed by Richard Farnsworth, William Dewsbury and others they wrote:

> Dearly beloved friends, these things we do not lay upon you as a rule or form to walk by, but that all with the measure of light which is pure and holy may be guided: and so in the light walking and abiding these may be fulfilled in the Spirit, not from the letter, for the letter killeth, but the Spirit giveth life.[2]

Many select meetings did not survive the persecution that was to follow.[3] Most of their members were imprisoned at one time or another, and many died there. Extremely bad conditions in the prisons killed many, and the plagues that affected the whole country killed others. The most notable remnants that did survive were two London meetings set up to oversee Friends work: the "Box Meeting" and the "Two Weeks Meeting". These had continued from their inception in 1656. A list of those who died in prison or from the plague is a list of the best known itinerant ministers. It includes: Thomas Aldam, John Audland, Edward Burrough, John Camm, Richard Hubberthorn, James Nayler, William Caton, Richard Farnsworth, Francis Howgill and many others. This loss of leadership resulted in a complete disruption of the elementary organization Friends had set up.

Friends suffered through successive waves of persecution. One particularly critical moment came during the Fifth Monarchy uprising. These men had seen the regicide of Charles I as a step to make Christ's Rule on earth possible. On Cromwell's death they only hoped it would come about. However, Charles II's restoration to the throne was seen as a denial of all their efforts and they rose in rebellion.

Friends had been identified with the people who had objected to the change, people who were socially and religiously very like them.

To avoid being identified with the Fifth Monarchists, Fox wrote his famous statement against all war, part of which reads:

Our principle is, and our practices have always been, to seek peace and ensure it and to follow after righteousness and the knowledge of God, seeking the good and welfare and doing that which tends to the peace of all. We know that wars and fightings proceed from the lusts of men (as Jas. iv. 1-3), out of which lusts the Lord hath redeemed us, and so out of the occasion of war. The occasion of which war and war itself (wherein envious men, who are lovers of themselves more than lovers of God, lust, kill, and desire to have men's lives or estates) ariseth from lust. All bloody   principles and practices, we, as to our own particulars, do utterly deny, with all outward wars and strife and fightings with outward weapons, for any end under any pretence whatsoever. And this is our testimony to the whole world.[4]

Political turmoil, changing legislation, wars and successive attempts by King Charles II to protect Catholics from Parliament had a profound effect on the persecution Friends experienced. It no longer involved imprisonment, but loss of property continued to be onerous. A respite of 1668 and 1669 gave Friends their chance to recover some of the losses. Thomas Ellwood wrote:

Not long after G. F. was moved of the Lord to travel through the countries, from county to county, to advise and encourage Friends to set up monthly and quarterly meetings, for the better ordering of the affairs of the church; in taking care of the poor; and exercising a true gospel discipline for a due dealing with any that might walk disorderly under our name; and to see that such as should marry among us did act clearly in that respect.[5]

The meetings that Fox set up recorded Friends sufferings, gave aid to the people in prison and their families, and kept records of births, marriages and deaths.

George Fox in a way almost incidental to his ministry began to "settle" general meetings.[6] This was one of his most important contributions to the Quaker movement. He would gather all Friends in an area and organize them into meetings. He found these organized meetings gave Friends a more settled manner for carrying on after him. His instructions were

That all do walk in Truth and righteousness and walk in holiness which becomes the house of God, and that all come to order their conversations alright...And they shall see the government of Christ who has all power in heaven and earth given to him,... But his government and order will remain...[7]

He added that:

... the Power of God is the Authority of all your men's and women's meetings ...[8]

However, the details of selecting a Friend to keep the minutes, the ordering of an agenda and the like came in gradually as Friends were moved to record them.

In 1671, Fox urged all monthly meetings to set up women's meetings. Although women had taken part in regular meetings, their part was becoming minor. He also arranged for several standing committees that were called meetings. One, the Six Weeks Meeting started in 1671, was a joint meeting of men and women leaders in London. Another, the Second Day Morning Meeting, was composed of traveling ministers in London. That meeting, later renamed more simply the Morning Meeting, eventually became the London Yearly Meeting publications committee. The most famous meeting of them all, the Meeting for Sufferings, was set up in October, 1675. It grew out of the conference called by the Morning Meeting to find relief from oaths and tithes and to "secure redress from sufferings."

Trying to overcome the effects of persecution, however, was not Friends only serious problem. After James Nayler, no one caused them as much pain, trouble and dissension as did John Perrot. He had been "convinced of the truth" in Ireland in 1655. He traveled in England and on the Continent preaching, and making contacts. While traveling on the Continent he felt called to "convince" the Pope. He set out for Rome with John Luffe. The Inquisition imprisoned them in the prison for madmen. John Luffe died there. Perrot survived and was released about the end of May, 1661.[9]

Perrot was given a warm welcome when he got back to England. His ideas were similar to Nayler's, which led him into conflict with George Fox. He felt that nothing should be done that was without the leadings of the Holy Spirit. He refused to remove his hat for prayers when he did not trust the spiritual leadings of those praying. However, what upset Friends was his feeling that the Spirit should also set the time for worship. To do otherwise was as wrong as attending the local "steeple house."[10]

Perrot's stand threatened the one thing that held Friends together: their habit of gathering for worship at set times and in set places. Fox, and others, felt that the key issue here was the need to stand together in public against the Conventicle Acts. By insisting on meeting only when the Spirit moved everyone, there would be times without meeting. Perrot held his views so strongly that Rufus Jones wrote:

> ... he pushed the testimony against form and ceremony to the absurd extreme of nihilism — there were to be no forms, not even the 'form' of holding meetings for worship ...[11]

Thomas Ellwood in reporting on John Perrot wrote:

> ... The reports of his great sufferings were ... joined with a singular show of sanctity ... made way for more ready propagation of that peculiar error of his, of keeping on the hat in time of prayer as well public as private unless they had an immediate motion at that time to put it off ... I amongst the many were caught in that snare..."

What John Perrot wrote was fairly persuasive:

> I told thee that it was that which the Lord required of me; if I should do otherwise, then I should sin: and therefore in as much as the Unity of the Saints, stood not in an Hat, or an outward Action with the Hat, but in the Spirit only; every Man walking according to the motions and guidings of it: for me to do a thing contrary to the motion of the Spirit, and thereby to sin against my God ... [12]

The harsh treatment given him by Fox rallied James Nayler's old supporters and added to the importance of Perrot's stand.[13]

Perrot had alienated many by the time he was arrested and committed to Newgate Prison for attending meeting. He further distanced himself by accepting voluntary exile to Barbadoes. At first, Friends on the island received him warmly. Later, when he went to Virginia and Maryland, Friends rejected him. In 1664 he accepted a post as Captain of the coast-watch and began wearing a sword which discredited him permanently in Friends eyes. He died in debt in Jamaica in 1665.[14]

The controversy of the "Hat," because Perrot had refused to remove his hat when other Friends prayed, did not divide Friends into separate groups. Perrot had received little support in the North, where the re-organization was just beginning. In the South, the dispute continued until 1666 when his followers were either reconciled or withdrew. In Maryland, there was a renewal of the controversy in 1672-4 that was equally serious. Reconciliation came as the result of a new phase of Quakerism everywhere.

A second conflict over the issues of central control of policy, the place of women in the movement, and the problems of internal discipline was much more threatening to the movement. Two important groups were involved. One group appeared in Preston Patrick, the "mother church" of the Seekers Fox had met in 1652. Two well-known First Publishers of the Truth, John Wilkinson and John Story, were at the center of the disagreement. They were both eventually to be found on Ernest Taylor's list of the Valiant 60.[15] They feared informers and they wanted to hold their meetings away from their village, instead of openly in their own houses. Other cautious groups appeared in Bristol and Reading.[16] The disagreement on whether to meet openly or in secret caused great heartache and strained relations. Each side felt the other was misguided.[17]

The second point at which these people disagreed with Fox was on the place of women in the body of the Friends of the Truth. While Fox was trying to establish the monthly meetings he had recognized women's contributions and looked for ways to insure them.[18] Many women had made notable contributions, not the least of which was that made by Margaret Fell. She not only oversaw the Kendal fund, she also carried on the extensive correspondence that had gone far toward holding the First Publishers of the Truth together. The haven of her home, Swarthmoor Hall, as a place of rest and recuperation was another of her contributions. However, her importance and that of other women declined as they aged and as two decades of persecution took their toll.[19] The women leaders who died had not been replaced in leadership by younger women. The issue of women's meetings became particularly important at Reading. The elders at Reading were particularly opposed to women acting in any capacity in the affairs of their church. They were quite vocal about it. There were no women in Reading who were able to oppose them.

The Separatists were opposed to Fox on still another matter. The troubles with Perrot made Friends want to get rid of undisciplined behavior. London Friends had, therefore, sent out a number of disciplining letters to all Friends. Friends outside London felt this was too much centralization. They published an anonymous piece in 1673 attacking George Fox and other leading men at Devonshire House, the meeting house of London Friends. They complained about "... their Tyrranical and Persecuting Practices ..." They wanted to be allowed to meet on the moors and save the heavy fines that came from meeting in Friends houses. The dissidents also wanted to be allowed to pay tithes and avoid the heavy fines for not paying them. Finally, they felt that centering things in London was limiting the action of the Spirit in them.[20]

Robert Barclay entered the debate at yearly meeting in 1673 after his release from prison. In his "Anarchy of the Ranters and other Libertines" he makes the point for the discipline of the group:

> ... the Church, gathering, or assembly of God's people has power to examine, and call to account such as...owning the same faith with them, do transgress and in case of their refusing to hear, or repent, to exclude them from fellowship. God has a special regard to the judgment and sense of his people, thus orderly proceeding so as to hold such bond in heaven, whom they bind on earth, and such loosed in heaven whom they loose on earth ..[21],[22]

In 1675 the second Conventicle Act was reapplied. Preston Patrick Friends were reproved for their backsliding. Margaret Fell and William Penn calmed the disagreement but were not able to end the conflict. In April, the quarterly meeting declined the Wilkinson-Story party proposal that they be allowed to conduct their meetings for worship in a way that would not attract the attention of the authorities. So, in May the dissidents set up their own distinct business meeting.[23]

In Reading, in 1678, three dissident trustees handed the meeting property over to Thomas Curtis, the man who had largely underwritten it. He then became the sole owner over the strenuous objection of the fourth trustee. Both groups then held a meeting at the same time in the same building with their backs to each other. Not surprisingly, the attempt failed to remain peaceful. Possible compromise vanished when Thomas Curtis had the front door bricked up. It took until 1716 to heal the separation, thirty-five years later, when the two groups joined in building a new meeting house.[24]

When the Anglican Tories returned to power in 1681 the last major period of persecution against Friends began. On Charles II's death his Catholic brother took the throne. There had been doubt about the Catholicism of Charles but there was none on that of James II. James II's conflict with Parliament centered around this fact as Englishmen still had a fear of foreign, Catholic, interference. The Toleration Act and James II's Declaration of Indulgences were seen in very different lights by different people. The Act of Toleration in 1689 and the Declaration of Indulgences in 1688 ended the persecution of Friends. At the time more than one thousand Friends were released from prison.

Since then several subjects have remained unquestioned: the "official" understanding of women's place in the meeting for worship and in the affairs of Friends; the need to hold regular meetings for worship and for business in advertised, known and regular places; the authority of the meeting to reach decisions; and, its preeminence in spiritual matters over individual Friends. However, individuals have not lost their responsibility in spiritual matters. Committees and meetings have been added and others have been "laid down," renamed or modified, but as a whole the formal structure of the Society has survived all the stresses and strains largely unchanged since that time.

Fox's vision from the top of Pendle Hill of a "great people to be gathered"[25] had matured. Friends had become a small self-conscious sect of people who removed their hats in time of prayer and shook hands at the close of worship. The Spirit moved in Friends, but it did so regularly and in specifically designated times and places. James Nayler's experience had hurt Friends badly, and Perrot's hit at the same sore point. From these incidents Friends discovered they could not survive if all were allowed free reign for their individualism.

Friends theological unorthodoxy was based on their experience of the Inner Light — the immediate revelation of God to the believer. This unorthodox form of worship required regular periods of waiting in silence. Since all utterances made in times of worship are potentially immediate revelation, undisciplined utterances and behavior had to be controlled. Anything not "in the Light" was "eldered," i. e., sanctioned. This was done to prevent a re-occurrence of the problems Friends had had with Nayler and Perrot. Friends egalitarianism and a refusal to pay tithes came from their convictions about the leadings of the Spirit which is open to all. The same belief produced the refusal to remove hats, the use of "thee" and "thou" and the freedom of women to participate fully in the life of the church. Such behavior was expected from all Friends. Swearing oaths in court, oaths of allegiance to obtain positions in the Army, a University or the Government, was required by law. Refusals to do so meant that Friends could not use the courts, or obtain positions in any of the institutions just mentioned. Yet, the same set of Friends ideals forbade swearing of oaths because it allowed two standards of honesty, one in and the other out of court. Friends "in the Light" saw swearing as a violation of the integrity of that Light and contrary to the commands of Scripture, so they suffered willingly.

Once a form of behavior was defined as being in the Light, it became part of the expectations imposed on all Friends. Changed conditions could alter the logical link between revelation and

23

behavior, but once the behavior was fixed it tended to remain. (Perhaps the most obvious places this happened was in dress and language. In time, using "thee" and "thou" and simplicity of dress became Quaker trademarks. Friends then continued to use the old forms because they set Friends apart from the world.)

The conflict James II had with Parliament ended when Parliament invited William III and Mary to take the throne of England. William III's Toleration Act eased matters greatly for Friends. Imprisonment did increase again during times of war to peak at more than one hundred a year in each of 1692, 1693 and 1694. The rate of imprisonment declined dramatically when the Whigs return to power in 1694. After that Friends major offenses consisted of their refusal to swear oaths of allegiance and to pay tithes. Alterations to the Poll Act and the Affirmation Act of 1694 effectively ended persecution of Friends in Great Britain. Since then Friends have only suffered during times of war. Analyzing this period, Hugh Barbour suggests that:

> During the intense persecution after 1661, Quaker non-violence won the respect of England and was eventually the largest factor in bringing the nation to a policy of toleration ... Since the costly persecution of the 1660's ... England has always trusted its non-conformists. The principle of "loyal opposition ... was a Puritan and, above all, Quaker contribution.[26]

3

Creeds, Politics and Appeals: Keith's Contribution

When Charles II died in 1685, he left no heir and was succeeded by his Catholic brother James II. By then Friends had started to move to Pennsylvania in large numbers. Those who moved escaped the final period of intense persecution. Charles II's grant of Pennsylvania to William Penn paid off a debt the King owed William Penn's father. The grant would have been politically impossible if the Whigs had not been out of office for a short time. It was as if this time had been given to provide Friends with a refuge. Friends alliance with James II then gave them the time to become well established in Pennsylvania.

In Pennsylvania, Friends faced new problems and opportunities. They now had a harsher climate on the one hand and an open and agriculturally untouched wilderness on the other. Friends, free from imprisonment and distraints, were allowed to live up to their ideals. In Pennsylvania and East Jersey Friends had no oaths to swear or tithes to pay, nor was there an established clergy. Parliament, Presbyterians, Baptists and Anglicans were far away in New York and did not harass the Friends in East Jersey and Pennsylvania. New England Puritans could be avoided if Friends stayed out of Massachusetts. For the first time Friends were free to work out their own lives.

In East Jersey, a Quaker had been in power for a time. There authority was placed in the hands of the assembly "...to make and repeal laws, to choose a governor, or commissioner, to execute the laws during their pleasure..."[1] As early as 1674 West Jersey had also come into the hands of wealthy Friends: John Fenwick and Edward Byllynge. When Byllynge went bankrupt, Penn and his trustees rescued him with money they borrowed from the Fenwicks. When Charles II died, control of West Jersey moved out of the hands of Friends, over a conflict in titles and a change in the fortune of the Quaker proprietors.

In Pennsylvania, Friends were to remain politically powerful until 1756. The legal basis for the government of the colony was a charter that vested major control in the hands of the governor and his council. The council was endowed with major legislative, executive and judicial powers. The governor sat as the presiding officer with a triple vote. He held the sole power of appointment to the other proprietary, provincial and county positions. At first Penn and the wealthy Friends who had invested in the new colony had almost complete control. The system established by Penn was more rigidly hierarchical than that set up in West Jersey.[2] The hierarchical nature of the government was to become important in the anger some Friends were to have against the Pennsylvania magistrates.

At the time of the founding of Pennsylvania, Friends "Holy Experiment," there was a group of non-Friends who lived in the area south of Philadelphia. These people were not clear about their relationship to the new proprietor. They owed Penn no personal loyalty. More important, the area they lived in was exposed to pirates and French raiders.

The second factor to disrupt the happy plans came from the rapid growth of the new colony. About 8,000 settlers arrived in the period 1681 to 1685.[3] Philadelphia merchants benefited from the trade generated by the newcomers. Some effort was made to control and limit trade, but these attempts failed. Trade combined with open land to the West to change the nature of the relationships between "gentlemen" and all the other settlers.

In 1684, Penn was anxious to have the funds he knew he would need to deal with the political problems he would face on his return to England. He, therefore, completed a very profitable land sale. It was made hurriedly in a way that opened the door to land speculation. It alienated many Friends who saw the action as a violation of their principles. So, when he left, his political realm was in disorder. The council was left in charge to struggle for power with two other factions. One faction was composed of Friends and the other of the people from the southern counties. In Penn's absence, Thomas Lloyd, the Deputy Governor, replaced several of the original council members who had owed direct loyalty to Penn. Lloyd joined with the new members to wrest as much power as they could from Penn.

The Glorious Revolution had brought William III and Mary to the throne in 1688. Penn's previous alliance with James II made his relationship to William III quite precarious. Penn was now faced with problems on both sides of the Atlantic. He had to regain control of the colony and deal with political problems in England at the same time. He, therefore, replaced Lloyd with John Blackwell as governor.

Blackwell was an able man, but he was also a Puritan. In England Blackwell was seen as the right choice. However, in Pennsylvania it was a poor one. Blackwell was seen as a representative of the people who had persecuted and tortured Friends in England and hanged them in Massachusetts. Blackwell then demonstrated his shortcomings by his attempt to regain control of the governing council. He imprisoned a few members of council and forced Lloyd out of the council. This transformed Lloyd from principal opponent of the Assembly to its chief advocate. The public was aroused, which made it even harder for Blackwell, or Penn, to control. Penn was forced to back down, remove Blackwell and let the Lloyd faction regain control of the province.

Blackwell was not the only problem faced by the Quakers in government. They were also faced by war with France and with the Indians. The southern counties were exposed to attacks from the sea by French raiders. The people there feared that the pacifistic Quakers were unlikely to arm and defend them. So the southern counties seceded to form the colony of Delaware. As the Quakers also had lost political control in West Jersey, Friends in Pennsylvania now felt they were surrounded by hostile forces. Lloyd and company reacted to control their province as tightly as possible.

In this atmosphere of political inexperience, incompetence, land speculation, disharmony and commercial success recently frustrated by war, George Keith tried to refocus Friends lives on the spiritual values he felt were most important. Like Wilkinson and Story, Keith had been "convinced" early in the history of Friends, but quite unlike most Friends he had graduated in theology at the age of twenty. Keith is supposed to have helped Barclay when he wrote the *Apology*. Although there are questions about the influence on Barclay, Barclay and Keith were fellow Scotsmen and had traveled together. Keith had been appointed Surveyor General of East Jersey by Barclay.[4]

Keith travelled with William Penn, George Fox, and Robert Barclay to Europe in 1677. In the period 1678 to 1680 Keith was imprisoned several times. In 1682 he went to jail for teaching without a license in a Friends school. When he got out in 1684 he traveled to America to survey the border between East and West Jersey, a position Robert Barclay offered him. Keith was also given a nice piece of land. After he surveyed the line dividing East from West Jersey, a line that was never used, Keith became recognized as a person of consequence in the religious life of the colony. He moved to Pennsylania in 1689 to become the head of the Philadelphia Latin School. He was asked to compose the reply from Burlington Quarterly Meeting to the epistle from London Yearly Meeting. He had also become one of the more influential of the First Publishers of Truth.[5]

Because Friends were politically powerful, many non-Friends had asked for membership in the Society. Keith felt that membership was given to new members too easily. At the same time, he had become disturbed by the spiritual inadequacies of young Friends and wanted them to imitate the discipline of the early church. He felt that young Friends behavior was not up to the standards expected of the earlier Friends. So, he set out to get Friends to reexamine the meaning of their contact with the Spirit of God and their understanding of the nature of the Christ of the New Testament. Keith became convinced that new members and young people should be required to make an open declaration of faith before they were admitted into fellowship. He would have limited Quaker weddings to Friends who made such a declaration.

In 1689 Keith began to set out his ideas in a series of pamphlets. The first to appear was "The Fundamental Truths of Christianity." The next year he produced " A Plain Short Catechism" and "The Christian Faith of the People of God called Quakers." The last of these was written at the request of Rhode Island Yearly Meeting. They accepted the "Chatechism" as a statement of their faith. However, the Burlington-Philadelphia Yearly Meeting rejected the statement.

Keith's approach to Quakerism was diametrically opposed to Perrot's. Keith wanted a Quakerism more like orthodox Christian groups. Friends who had earlier rejected Perrot's teaching as "running out from the Truth," rejected Keith's ideas as "downright Popery." He was rebuffed at the yearly meeting in 1690 and again in 1691. The rebuff, and the laxity he saw among the governing group in Pennsylvania, caused him great distress.[6] Keith could not have chosen a more inauspicious time to introduce his "Catechism," or to begin an acrimonious discussion on the spiritual and moral short-comings of the Friends in power. Yet, he was clearly not alone. Others shared his concern and desired to do something about the sad state of the spiritual affairs of Friends.[7]

War and smuggling brought the matter to a head. One smuggler,

Babbit by name, stole a ship from the Philadelphia wharves. With it he raided the farms and towns along the Delaware River. When a group of armed non-Quaker men dealt with the situation, the people in power did nothing to stop them. Friends in power were helpless in the face of the violence. They had been barred by their ideals from using force to bring Babbit to justice. Keith objected to the Council's lack of action not because they failed to control piracy, but because they had allowed force to be used against the pirate.

> ... He found fault with his friends in the magistracy, and their execution of the penal laws against malefactors, as being inconsistent with their religious profession; and, in short, contended that he and such as joined with him, were the true Quakers, and all the rest, who opposed him were apostates ...[8]

The Magistrates were irritated by Keith's criticism of their spiritual laxity and their inability to govern morally. They remembered that Keith had received his appointment as master of the school in Philadelphia from Penn and that he had supported Governor Blackwell against them. The Magistrates, therefore issued "The Declaration, or Testimony, of Denial ..." against him. The statement was signed by Thomas Lloyd, then Governor of Pennsylvania, two members of the council, and by several magistrates who called themselves "The Meeting of Public Friends in Philadelphia." This interesting document dated the twentieth of Fourth month, 1692 begins with:

> Beloved Friends, In tender love, and with spirits bowed down before the Lord is this our salutation to you...

It goes on to accuse Keith of having:

> ... gone into a spirit of enmity, wrath and self-exaltation, contention and jangling: and, as a person without regard to his Christian brethren, and letting loose to an extravagant tongue, he hath broken out into many ungodly speeches, railing accusations, and passionate threatenings towards many of his brethren and elders; and that upon slender occasions. And, when some, in Christian duty, have laid before him his unsavory words, and abusive language, as a person of common civility would loath, it hath been too frequent him, and that, in a transport of heat and passion, to call some of his brethren, in the ministry and other elders, and that upon small provocation (if any) Fools, ignorant Heathen, Infidels, silly souls, Lyers, Heretics, rotten Ranters, Muggeltonians ...[9]

The conflict, which by now had involved most of the Friends in Pennsylvania and New Jersey, was carried to yearly meeting. There Keith defended himself and attacked his opponents. He withdrew with his supporters from the yearly meeting. Friends who remained wrote a minute against Keith and the Friends who withdrew with him. That minute was sent along with their Yearly Meeting Epistle to London Friends, with copies to all other Friends yearly meetings. Shortly after, George Keith was disowned by Friends in New England, Long Island, Maryland, Virginia and Barbados.

Keith replied to the indictment of the yearly meeting by publishing "The Plea of the Innocent," "The Appeal from Twenty-eight Judges" and "Some Reasons and Causes of the Late Separations." Two other Friends who supported him were brought before the court for publishing "The Appeal" without the permission of the magistrates and without the name of the publisher. William Bradford, who printed the book, and John McComb, who distributed it were found guilty and jailed. This is probably the only time when a Quaker was jailed by another Quaker for publishing the Truth as seen by a third Quaker.[10]

The year 1692 was a one of difficulties for everyone. The provincial government was taken away from Penn and a royal government was imposed. Yearly meeting held that year was a time of insults, mutual condemnations and recrimination. Keith and about one quarter of the members present withdrew in anger and were disowned.[11] The Friends who withdrew refused to accept the disownment because a large number of the Friends who had attended that yearly meeting — the group disowned — were not united with the verdict. When the disowned Friends returned to Philadelphia after yearly meeting, George Keith, William Bradford, Peter Boss and Thomas Budd were charged with defamation by the magistrates as a result of statements made in "A Plea for the Innocent." In their trial the defendants tried to establish the illegality of the proceedings. The jury refused to bring a verdict against Bradford. However, he was returned to jail for his earlier misdemeanors. Keith and Budd were fined five pounds each, which they never paid.[12]

The trial did not keep the disowned Friends from meetings for worship with the Friends who had disowned them. Keith persisted in his accusations of heresy. His opponents, in turn, tried to prove *he* was the heretic. He was assaulted and refused access to the speakers gallery in one meeting for worship.

One Sunday morning a meeting discovered speakers' galleries at both ends of their meeting house, the second one built by Keith's supporters. Keith had been refused his request for a seat on the speaker's gallery, something he had been invited to on early occasions. The elders' refusal infuriated Keith's supporters enough to cause them to build the new gallery just so Keith could have a place to speak from. The elders, who were also magistrates, were angry and had the new gallery torn down. In their frustration, Keith's supporters destroyed the old gallery. The monthly meeting condemned both parties and the separation became complete.

Keith's followers organized their own meetings and called themselves the "Christian Quakers." They began a thorough examination of their relationship to the State and the conditions of the world around them. In keeping with their idealism, in their monthly meeting held October, 1693, they produced "An Exhortation and Caution to Friends Concerning Buying and Keeping Negroes," the first Friends published statement against owning slaves.

At about this time Keith wrote and published "Truth Advanced in the Correction of Many Gross and Hurtful Errors." Although the altruism of the "Exhortation" came to be shared by most Friends, the theological doctrines of "Truth Advanced" have been rejected. Keith's ideas had changed by this time and were outside the limits that could be accepted by Friends. With his departure to England in 1693, the split between the Quakers and the Christian Quakers became permanent. His intention to reform and the religious, political and personal differences produced a new sect.

The charges made against Keith for his " ... overbearing temper and unChristian disposition of mind ... "[13] were paralleled by equally unChristian charges made by his supporters. Both sides were angry and both had reason for their anger.[14] He was accused of apostasy and the ambition of becoming Fox's replacement[15] and of having become deranged.[16] However, he had only changed his theological position and persuaded a large contingent of Friends to accept it.[17] He also had challenged the political and ministerial authority of the elders.[18] When the majority refused to accede to his view, he was short tempered and contentious about it. It was at this time that the controversy became political. He simply looked further for additional ammunition.[19]

In England, Keith appealed his disownment to London Yearly Meeting. Penn sided with him at first but later found this hard to do. The Second Day's Morning Meeting, which was the publications committee for London Yearly Meeting, investigated the matter and judged against him. He appealed to the Six Weeks Meeting, the meeting of public Friends in London, and they referred the matter to the yearly meeting. The yearly meeting gave the matter a great deal of prayerful thought. They concluded, in part, that the magistrates should not have meddled in the matter. They criticized Keith for his false ideas, counseled him, and left the matter in God's hands. By this action they defined the issue as a fundamentally religious one. They thus denied the entire political dimension the discussion had in Philadelphia. The redefinition was retained by most historians until Nash reemphasized the importance of politics once again.

The yearly meeting asked Keith to withdraw his published attacks against Quakers. To this end he published: "The Causeless Ground of Surmises, Jealousies and Unjust Offenses Removed." Unfortunately, other things had gone too far. Keith was unable to stop himself or his supporters. A "True Account of the Proceedings...at the Yearly Meeting..., to which is added an Account of the Yearly Meeting at Burlington...showing the Disharmony of the two said Meetings... (London, 1694)" appeared. In it Friends were accused of trying to cloak "the Anti-Christian Errors, and persecuting Practice of their Apostate Brethren in Penn-Sylvania..." This was the last straw. He was now deserted by all his old friends, including those in his home meeting in Aberdeen. He tried meeting with some of the schismatic Friends from earlier separations but got little support from them.

At the yearly meeting in 1695 he was disowned. For a while he tried and failed to retain contact with Friends on his own terms. In time his preaching brought him support from the Anglican Church. After Keith left he saw Quakers as victims of false philosophical principles. They were victims of errors that had been present in the movement from the beginning.[20] Theologically by this time Keith had developed ideas that were very orthodox. According to Endy, Keith felt it was the "...height of arrogance for Quakers to assert that they know not only what God provides ... but the principle by which he does it."[21] Friends now treated Keith as an enemy who deserved only to be attacked. Since then he has never been given credit for the work he did in the early years for Friends. His former supporters, the Christian Quakers in Philadelphia, were deeply hurt by his abandonment of them when he joined the Anglican Church. They gradually fell apart and most of them joined other religious bodies.[22]

The break was important in both England and America. It took on quite different forms on each side of the Atlantic. In Pennsylvania and New Jersey it had involved a Quaker government and an attempt to purify the religious basis of the Society. In Britain it was, in essence, the disownment of a long-time and well-known Friend who had changed his beliefs sufficiently to no longer fit in with other members of the Society. He was dealt with at great length because he had suffered and been imprisoned for his Quaker beliefs. Politics were important in both places. However, in England the politics were purely religious politics. Political conditions were so different in the two places that the separation had to take on different forms and have different meanings.

In England the conflict was regarded as very serious but, by nature, largely a religious disagreement. Keith was grouped with all the others who had, at one time or another, lost contact with the Light. In America, however, the conflict was the first large division between groups of Friends. There, the combination of religious differences, political disagreements and a challenge to the Friends in positions of political and ministerial power, and wealth came to bear on what happened.[23] The bonds of family and friends that served so well to hold English Friends together failed to do so in Pennsylvania and New Jersey. When the strain of religious discord[24] was added to the conflict over treatment of pirates, the system broke down. In Pennsylvania and New Jersey a separation of a large group took place, while in England Keith was an isolated individual. The theological disagreement was similar in both places, but the break with a large group only took place when the disagreement involved several other coinciding issues. If there is any obvious point that can be made here, it is that while Friends can disagree on theological points all they want, to combine these with other issues, especially ones involving power, leaves them in danger of a schism.

The long-term effect of these events is very hard to measure. Friends rejected Keith and his followers and were quite at a loss to explain his actions. The explanations ran all the way from insanity to an ambition to replace George Fox as the most influential Friend. His group of followers disappeared. His devotion to work in the Anglican Church only left Friends feeling they were right in having disowned him.

4

The
Eighteenth Century

During the first half of the eighteenth century England prospered in relative peace. Friends came to be seen as normal religious dissenters as their political alliance with Catholics disappeared. Thus, Friends were no longer dangerous to the people in power.

At the turn of the eighteenth century English Friends were still a remnant that suffered from persecution, albeit in a greatly limited form. Some Friends continued to refuse to pay tithes or to swear oaths, so the authorities arrested and fined them. As Friends would not pay these fines, their goods were seized and sometimes they were imprisoned. Once in awhile a Friend would die tragically in prison. The Affirmation Act that allowed Friends to affirm and not swear was renewed and finally made perpetual in 1715. In 1722 it was extended to allow Friends to initiate court action and testify in criminal cases. The Corporation Act and the Test Act still kept Friends out of government posts, professions and universities. So, Friends became successful in industry, trade, science and medicine.

As Friends moved into the towns and cities they became a self-conscious body. Their practices of care for each other under persecution were extended. They apprenticed young Friends to older ones, to ensure both their livelihood and their spiritual growth. When the industrial revolution changed the system of apprenticeships, Friends continued to work with other Friends.[1] Friends who traveled on business affairs found ways to combine this with their ministry, which also helped draw Friends together into one body.

Enclosure in a small social group had its compensations. Meetings for business involved travel and the need for overnight accommodation recurred regularly. Friends were inevitably invited into each other's homes. Contacts made and remade over many years held them together in ways we now would find hard to appreciate.[2]

The issues that divided Friends earlier had been resolved; for the time being they were "in unity." Their main concerns were for their spiritual message and each other's welfare. The Friends message had to be kept clear, so much of their effort went into writing down their practices. They felt it would allow them to conduct the business of their meetings peacefully and keep their lives in the Light.[3]

Persecution had removed the uncommitted and had taught Friends to care for each other. The financial problems of persecuted Friends had caused the Kendal Fund to be established half a century earlier. The Kendal Fund had quickly shown itself to be inadequate to care for all Friends in distress, so other funds were started. By the early eighteenth century the care provided by the funds was used to care for any Friend in financial distress. Local governments in England refused to care for any non residents. As England industrialized, many people were forced to migrate and often faced financial distress. Friends were only a small part of this stream. Like other urban immigrants, they were not considered to be residents and were given no help by their new localities. Friends did have a mechanism to help each other. The care they gave each other attracted "non-members." As a result, some meetings began to look for ways to limit their support to those who were judged to be in membership. The first mention of a discussion of this at the yearly meeting level was in 1693.[4]

In 1737 London Yearly Meeting drew up a minute that formally defined membership for the first time to solve the problem of too many indigent people. It limited Friends responsibilities to care for Friends and their children.[5] The minute solved the problem but also it created a new form of membership. For the first time children acquired membership by right of parent's conviction, hence birthright membership. Later the new form of membership was to help the Society of Friends to survive. However, in the process, Friends lost the select nature of the meetings for church affairs. Before, only the "well-seasoned" had been invited to them. With formal membership all Friends, including children who grew up as Friends, were free to attend meetings for business.

With convinced Friends and birthright Friends, their meetings found clear distinctions in the contribution they made. The differences in spiritual gifts made Friends look for another way to recognize the distinctions. A partial answer was a Yearly Meeting of Elders that began in 1754. Gifts in the ministry were recorded for the first time at the yearly meeting level in 1773.

Friends faced change in other ways. Urban and overseas migration had greatly changed the size and composition of meetings. New meetings had come into existence. Many old meetings had either declined greatly in size or had simply vanished. In their attempts to regulate change, Friends had gradually added rules and procedures. By 1738, Friends began to keep a list of Extracts from their minutes to keep track of the rules. The Extracts were compiled, and copies were made for all monthly meetings. By 1750 the need for large scale change in the Society of Friends had become obvious. In 1768 Friends redefined the bounds of monthly and preparative meetings to bring representation into line with membership.

Most reforms in London Yearly Meeting came in times of peace. Membership was defined and the Extracts were copied in 1737 and 1738 just before the start of the war with Spain in 1739. The final effort to change the Affirmation Act to make it acceptable by Friends came in 1749, after the war with Spain and before the start of the Seven Years War. Recording ministers at the yearly meeting level came in 1773. The Advices were printed in 1783 just after the Treaty of Versailles ended the war with France. The Book of Extracts was printed in 1802 during the two year lull in the Napoleonic wars.

The few changes made in time of war included: the creation of the Yearly Meeting of Elders and printing the marriage rules, in 1754. The revision of the Queries came the year after. The practice of writing answers to the Queries before each quarterly meeting began at that time. These all took place during the French and Indian War — one that was far removed from Friends in Great Britain. The other exception was the reform of the monthly meetings in 1768, the only major change in the Society of Friends in Great Britain to take place at time of war.

The second half of the century saw important economic and social changes. The Seven Years War and then the wars with France were to pit England against the world for an "endless" period of time. In addition, the supply of firewood gave out so a new form of fuel had to be found. Coal came into its own as did mines, canals, and, eventually, railroads. Friends were in a good position to take advantage of these changes. Their exclusion from government and the universities had allowed them to build some very impressive enterprises. Many Friends had become quite wealthy in the process.[6]

By mid-century Friends were becoming a "peculiar people." "Plain" dress and speech set them apart. Refusal to swear set them further apart. Attendance at mid-week meeting for worship was required; the employers most ready to allow this were other Quakers. Marriage to non-Quakers usually led to disownment, not just for those who married but for those who helped the marriage take place. These practices grew out of Friends convictions and were as much a part of their religion as was their opposition to war, slavery, tithing and drunkenness. All Friends practices were intended to protect and to keep them uncontaminated by the world.

Wealthy Friends, by now an important group even outside the Society, had troubles with these limitations. They were the ones who were most frequently tempted by the world. Daniel Quare, for one, resisted great temptation. He refused to accept the title of "Clock and Watchmaker" to the King in 1714. The title would have been an important and lucrative position. His reason: "...I did see no way to accept and enjoy since I could not Qualifie my self according to Law..."[7] He would have been required to swear an oath of loyalty to accept the title.

The work of George Whitefield and John Wesley and the Sunday School Movement, which began in England in the 1780s, raised questions of evangelism, revivals and immediate salvation in Friends minds. Although Friends took to the idea of the Sunday Schools with enthusiasm, the theological issues were slow to affect them. Whitefield's and Wesley's efforts also increased the numbers of dissenters in the country. As Friends joined with these dissenters who shared their social concerns, they were opened to their new religious ideas.

The wealthy and influential Friends who had the most contact outside the Society were the first to take to the new evangelical ideas. The drive and profound knowledge of the Bible of early Friends had been dissipated. The new ideas required a return to biblical learning. Beginning again to study the Bible carried a number of other ideas, ideas that echoed the Keithian division. The ideas created a strain between Friends that was to be tested very early in the next century. Fortunately, however, Friends in England were a very tightly knit body of people. They worked for and with each other in many different realms, not the least of which was the one that maintained their Society of Friends.

B. North America

North America was both far away and vastly different from England.

It was an extensive open land with none of the ancient and customary rights to determine its use; it was a wilderness where new things were possible. There was enough land for all, and too much for any single group to control. The first people to travel from England to the New World had arrived many years before the first Friends. They had removed many of its unknowns and so reduced the gamble of moving there. However, Friends still had to face the problems of climate, distance and sickness.

Sickness, of concern on both sides of the Atlantic, claimed hundreds in several epidemics. The colonies were much more sparsely settled and, hence, did not have the same kind of problem with plagues that the people in Europe did. When plagues did strike the colonies they were the result of illness that was brought to them from Europe by ship. The most devastating problem they faced in their colonies was, therefore, closely tied to the problems of distance.

In the eighteenth century the distance between England and her North American colonies took weeks to overcome. Travel from one side of the Atlantic to the other was both limited and expensive. The number of Friends who traveled from England was never very high, except in the early period of the Pennsylvania colony. Later, the number of Friends per decade who crossed the Atlantic both ways to minister to those on the other side exceeded twenty only during the 1730s, 1750s and 1790s — an average of but two Friends per year. Once across, they stayed for a long time. On their return to England, or to America if they had started there, they carried on long correspondence with the Friends they had left behind. Traveling Friends did not solely start in England. One of the best known traveling Friends, John Woolman, had started his work in New Jersey and ended it when he died in York. So, the effect of the travel was greater than the frequency might suggest.

Friends on both sides of the Atlantic kept accounts of their spiritual journeys in "journals." The deceptive similarity between journal accounts of English and American Friends disguises different physical conditions. The accounts do not show that Friends in the Colonies traveled less frequently than did those in England. Colonial Friends did not have the means or freedom to travel as easily and Colonial distances were enormously greater than those in England. Also, most Colonial Friends were farmers who were tied to their land and could only travel in winter.

The mini-ice age of the mid eighteenth century, in a curious way, may have encouraged colonial Friends to travel in winter. Chalkley reports ice on the Delaware and ships frozen up in Philadelphia in

1731-32. If this happened near the ocean, the swamps and streams inland must also have frozen, allowing for easy travel on them. (Frozen water served as the highways for Friends until very recently in Canada. Older Friends today still remember tales told by their parents of easy travel over frozen ground.)

Wealth and power also complicated Friends' lives in the colonies. At one time or another, and for varying lengths of time, Friends held power in four of the thirteen colonies. To Pennsylvania one should add West Jersey, Rhode Island and North Carolina.[8] Friends ruled in Pennsylvania from the first years until 1756. It was the longest period of time Friends controlled any of the colonies. In North Carolina and West Jersey the time they governed was quite short. Yet, the effect of their short time in power on West Jersey has been profound.

The first serious struggle between Friends convictions and their desire to remain in political power came in 1701. At that time the Governor of Pennsylvania demanded men and money to protect the Colony against foreign attack. This demand was repeated in 1709 and in 1711. Each time the Quakers in the Pennsylvania Assembly voted funds to the Queen for the support of her government. Thus they protected both their testimony against war and their political power. In 1710, Philadelphia Yearly Meeting cautioned the Assembly about deviating from Friends principles. Opposition to warlike activities was less important at the time to important Friends than political power.[9]

For the next thirty years Friends enjoyed the same kind of peace enjoyed by those in Britain. However, because they were in political power American Friends had many more upsets than did English Friends. Friends governed Pennsylvania, developed their fortunes and their discipline with many alarms but no major interruptions. During this time Friends became outnumbered in Pennsylvania by non-Friends. In the process they found themselves faced with changes in behavior of the people around them that drove them to distraction.[10] At the end of the thirty years they had lost much of their interest in education and had begun to disown people for marrying out.[11] They also began to migrate west in greater numbers.[12]

In the turmoil of political change, immigration, new groups to contend with, and wars, the free open land to the west gave hope that personal conditions could always be improved. The adventure and excitement of building something new and potentially valuable drew people to it. Friends may have taken more time to consider migrating than did non-Friends, but this did not stop them. They went as individuals, in groups, and sometimes as whole communities. Before leaving, however, they made their peace with their consciences and other Friends.

The colonies were faced with war again in 1739, and the Pennsylvania Assembly was asked to provide money and arms. The Assembly, after a series of long and contentious sessions, decided to vote three thousand unsolicited pounds for the King's use as a substitute for the war taxes for which they had been asked. They also suggested that the governor was within his rights to raise a militia. They said that those who felt moved to defend themselves militarily had the right to do so, probably because they feared charges of treason. Respect was, however, to be given those who objected to taking part in warlike activities.[13] At that time John Kinsey was Speaker of the Assembly, leader of the Quaker party and Clerk of Philadelphia Yearly Meeting. Very few other Quakers have combined so much authority at one time. In opposition to him were some younger Friends who rejected the idea of a militia and the compromise.

Politically, Friends in Pennsylvania were divided into three groups. One group was concerned with governing the colony to the best of its abilities and with maintaining political power. A second group became concerned with moral laxity and felt a need to remove Friends from power altogether. A third group wanted to apply Friends principles to the exercise of power. The three groups formed coalitions in various ways right up to the Revolutionary War.[14]

Pennsylvania Friends political differences were highlighted by the French and Indian War. Land fraud and territorial invasions led to an attack by the Indians. Many Friends felt the Indians were justified in their aggression. After the initial attack by the Indians, the governor demanded taxes to pay for the colony's defense. The wealthy and politically powerful Friends were faced by an idealistic opposition. The Governor's demands to raise taxes for defense created enormous dissension. And, the Assembly could no longer make the compromises it had made earlier.

In the election of 1756 held only weeks after the governor had declared war on the Indians, only twelve Friends were elected to office. There had been twenty-six Friends in the thirty-six member House before the election. Four of the newly elected Friends were persuaded not to take their seats. For the first time, Friends did not make a majority in the Assembly. They were never to do so again.

The two issues of Indians and war preparations bedeviled Friends even further in 1764. The Paxton Boys attacked and murdered a group of Christian Indians. The Paxtons had threatened to march on and do the same to another Indian group. Some younger Friends, who feared for the safety of the Indians, combined to defend them. No battle took place but the defenders did use a Friends meeting house without permission during a rain storm. The young Friends were "dealt with" but no one was disowned for his part in the activities. Perhaps they were simply given a good scolding.[15]

The nature of the constitution and representation in Parliament were two political issues which complicated life for Friends in the colonies. Most of the members of Parliament in London saw the constitution as the product of the laws passed, laws that could be amended at will. Opposed to this view was the idea that the constitution should incorporate human rights that transcended Parliament, and should serve as a guide for writing laws.

Furthermore, although Parliamentarians were elected by ridings, most Members of Parliament did not see themselves as representatives of their ridings (political districts). They were chosen and elected in a way that made them feel a debt of obligation to their class and to the country, rather than to the electors of their ridings. In their debates Parliamentarians saw themselves as looking after the welfare of all the King's subjects rather than the welfare of their electors. New political ideas raised questions about both of these views. Opposition to this view came from the disenfranchised in both England and the Colonies.

The view held by the disenfranchised was to the effect that Parliamentarians should be accountable to their electors and should look after their electors' interests. Suffrage was not universal for men — women's suffrage was to be debated at a later date — which caused a large measure of the discomfort. Slavery was the term used to broadly define deprivation of representation in government. Chattel slavery did not become an issue until much later as it was a practice that was rejected at the time by only a few, mostly Quakers. They, thanks to the efforts of dedicated souls such as John Woolman, had almost freed themselves of slave holding by the last third of the century.

Equality became part of the new baggage of political ideas under discussion. Deference to wealth, nobility and royalty was rejected. The idea of an established Church was brought into question. Friends, and many others, felt that the Anglican Church, the Church of England, should not be the established church just as the Puritan Church, which was established in Massachusetts, should also be rejected.[16]

The debate on these ideas was part of the context in which the events in the latter part of the eighteenth century were to develop.

41

Friends were in unity only on their rejection of an established church. For Friends in Pennsylvania there were some additional problems. Some of the wealthiest merchants were Friends. Just before the American Revolution the problems became more serious when the wealthy became wealthier and the poor became more numerous. It was not the first time it had happened. On the whole Friends were better off than the rest of the population, if only because many of the wealthiest were Friends. Much of the wealth was generated by trade that was protected by the Navy. The Imperial Government felt that the wealth generated should, therefore, be taxed and controlled. The Stamp Act and the Townshend Act were passed to these ends. Wealthy Friends now found themselves in the middle of the political debate. On the one hand, they had scruples about war and, on the other, they wanted to go on trading. Like many others, they too objected to the imposition of taxes by a government they could not influence.[17]

As in England, North American Friends became more self-conscious as they were affected by the religious renewal around them. This self-consciousness re-awakened interest in Friends traditional testimonies and emphasized the undesirable compromises politics required. George Whitefield made a trip through New England and New Jersey in 1739. Friends were not attracted to listen to him, but they were affected by his work with non-Friends. Friends began to re-evaluate their own convictions. They became more regular in their attendance at meeting for worship and showed an increase in their desire for reform.

The ministers and elders were caught in a bind. On the one hand they were made increasingly conscious of their convictions and identity. On the other hand, the westward movement exposed them to the outside world and gave young Friends more choices for marriage partners outside the Society. This brought the rate of disownment up from ten per year to over 750 per year by 1760.[18]

Between 1774 and 1776 the hostilities purified Friends witnesses on several issues. During the war Friends showed their religious mettle even though progress in ethics was uneven. The majority refused to pay war taxes. They, therefore, remained clear of violations of the Discipline. However, there was a mixture in motives in the stand Friends took toward the question of the payment of war taxes. Some Friends who appeared scrupulous refused not for the sake of conscience but out of a fondness for the old regime. On the demands to swear oaths, however, Friends remained firm. Any compromise on participation in the war came to be generally deplored. All Friends who weakened and took part were dealt with and disowned. The disowned Friends formed their own society of Free Quakers.[19]

The cost of the hostilities to Friends was, first of all, the loss of membership of those who fought. They were disowned. Trying to remain aloof from the war eroded Friends political influence further. At the same time Friends were alienated from both revolutionaries and loyalists. Later some of the more prominent Friends were banished because they had supported the British.[20]

When the hostilities ended some Friends migrated to Canada and others moved to England. Technically those who left were not loyalists, nor were those who stayed behind revolutionaries. Both groups had refused to fight. In time they were able to re-integrate themselves and maintain bonds with those who left. The bonds allowed American Friends to help establish the earliest meetings in Canada.[21]

After the war North American Friends interests and concerns were far more like those of Friends in Britain. The work they did in education and philanthropy were very similar. Friends philanthropy was consistent with their withdrawal from society. They showed their benevolence toward the Blacks, both free and slave, and to the Indians.[22] American Friends were like English Friends in that they "...ceased to prophecy in public against steeple houses, and had become a thrifty dealer studying to be quiet..."[23] By the end of the century Friends practices had become "testimonies." Among them were: the use of "plain" speech, which included absolute honesty and the use of "thee" and "thou"; the requirement to attend mid-week meeting for worship; and, the now important ones that prohibited slave holding, warlike activities, gambling, alcohol consumption and swearing. Other prohibitions were aimed at music, dancing and the long standing one against a "hireling" ministry. Some of the testimonies had deep spiritual meaning and some merely kept Friends a "peculiar people." Whatever the spiritual meaning, the outward effect was evident: Friends dressed, spoke and acted in ways that separated them from the world.[24]

C. Loss of Members

During the eighteenth century there was little persecution, and there were no large divisions between Friends. Worship was the focus of their membership, and worship was generally silent. However, life was not quiet in other ways. Friends disowned each other, withdrew from meetings and moved away from their meetings in large numbers. Disownments were common in all the yearly meetings, and represent the greatest loss of members in Quaker history.

At the outbreak of the American revolution there were an estimated thirty thousand members in Philadelphia Yearly Meeting. Between 1748 and 1783 a total of just under thirteen thousand had been reported as delinquents to a monthly meeting of whom about 6,770 were disowned. The greatest single cause of loss was due to marriage delinquency. The second most frequent cause was disownment of 908 Friends for participation in revolutionary activities.[25]

During the period of the 1720s to the 1760s the rates of marrying out increased from a minority to a majority. In Philadelphia Yearly Meeting, the total number of Friends brought to the attention of their monthly meetings for marriage delinquency alone was 4,925, of whom about 46 percent were disowned. How many recanted and returned, and how many others simply drifted off, will probably never be determined.[26] Other reasons given for disowning members included the offenses of gambling, drunkenness, financial insolvency, pride and vanity (e.g. having objectionable clothes or furnishings), dancing, singing and whistling, violating First Day, fraud, theft, usury, smuggling, tax evasion, deceit, and revolutionary activities.

There was one disownment in 1758, however, that did not fit the pattern of what is essentially sacrilege. Instead it was a disownment for heresy, something that was both more serious and the first warning of future problems. This was the disownment of John Bartram by Darby Monthly Meeting in Pennsylvania. The minute states:

> ... That [due to] his disbelief in the divinity of our Lord and Saviour Jesus Christ as being perfectly God as well as man ... we hereby declare the said John Bartram to be no member of our Christian Society ..[27]

John Bartram's disownment was important for its prediction of the future. The cessation of persecution had combined with a decline in an educated leadership early in the century[28] and the developing dominance of the elders as guardians of tradition to produce a period of Quaker Quietism. Out of it came a complete dependence on the Inward Light as the source of inspiration, to the neglect of Bible teaching.[29] As described by Elbert Russell, Quaker Quietism is a form of mysticism in which God can work through sinful and spiritually incapacitated people only when "activities of the 'creature' are 'quiet'." According to him, Quietism came from: a) Barclay's combination of the doctrine of "human depravity and of the universal and saving Light;" b) "the lingering effect of Ranterism;" c) the religious relaxation and d) cessation of early evangelism.[30] Until the evangelization of the wealthy Quaker leaders, Quietism was the dominant religious form for the Society of Friends.

During the seventeenth century Friends had created a relatively small and tightly knit sect separated from the world. Its members were all convinced of the Truth of their basic message. The century saw the clarification of their belief system and the creation of the social system necessary to perpetuate it. Membership had been confined to those who had been "baptized in the Truth." Thus, they were limited to adults and to those children mature enough to understand. Although the message was intended for everyone, only those who had fully accepted it by facing persecution were welcomed to the inner "select meetings."

In Pennsylvania, Friends had refused to allow Quakerism to become the established religion. Friends permitted religious freedom, as demanded in principle by their belief in the Inward Light.[28] Yet, because of the nature of Penn's grant, Friends were obliged to take on the responsibilities of government and the development of the economic life of Pennsylvania. In England Friends carried on the tasks which ensured the life of their sect. Membership was defined permanently. They clarified the discipline and established the roles of ministers, elders and overseers.

With growth of the discipline and religious self-awareness, some Friends began to understand the conflict between their traditional ideals and their wealth and political power. Events in 1739, 1755 and 1756 highlighted the conflict. The politically active Friends in Pennsylvania would have transformed their religion into something quite different to the Quakerism practiced outside Pennsylvania. The compromises they were willing to take would have transformed Quakerism into a denomination very like the others.

In contrast, there was a group of reformers who were closer to the Quaker mainstream. The reformers were Friends who were troubled by the compromises taken with historical Quaker ideals. They fought against the politically active Friends who were willing to accept compromises to retain power. The politically active Friends were willing to sacrifice the elements Friends had, traditionally, thought to be important. Visiting English Friends reinforced the reformers at a critically important moment in 1756. Politically active Friends faced an election that put great strain on Friends principles. As the visitors carried the prestige of the "mother" yearly meeting, their intervention was extremely important. Friends ideals won out. Never since has the possession of political power been central to Friends concern.

Power combined with wealth delayed facing the contradictions between politically active Friends and the Quaker ideals. The politically powerful Friends, who were central to the yearly meeting, developed arguments that allowed them to carry on. When their compromises violated the strongest feelings of the majority of Friends, most of them chose the Society Friends over political power.

The coincidence of the migration to new lands and the effect of the Great Spiritual Awakening on the Friends discipline were devastating. Just when young Friends had problems in their quest for new marriage partners, the elders felt forced to disown them for marrying the only available acceptable candidates. Yet, had the elders done otherwise, they would have been the object of discipline for laxity. The result was the huge loss of members and an increase in the numbers of former Friends who had a reason to be angry with the elders.

Once Friends had withdrawn from political life, subsequent events strengthened the discipline and Friends convictions. The elders were then able to deal more easily with delinquents who acted outside the Light. Further purification brought on by the war strengthened traditional testimonies on peace and social reform. The Society of Friends was opened permanently to contacts with those who shared their concerns. The openness strengthened work on freeing the slaves, reinforced concern for education, continued the work with Indians and the poor, and, in general, stimulated Friends philanthropic spirit. New concerns were soon added in the form of work for prison reform and for the humane treatment of the insane.

The social costs of reform and war went beyond the loss of members through disownment. The intimate nature of the Society of Friends and its domination of members' lives has often been described. For the disowned the loss was of religion, friends and even family. They ceased being Quakers and had to find a new religion, one they may have scorned earlier. The hurt probably added to those who later looked for revenge against the remaining Friends for their non-alignment during the revolution.

The Century
of Separations

5

Theology Returns: Philadelphia Divides

After the Revolutionary War American Friends slowly rebuilt their lives. The few who had been banished returned to their homes to begin again. Some had moved on to Canada or gone back to England. The majority, however, had remained where they were. The ones who had fought had been disowned and lost to Quakerism. Those remaining in the Society were, then, more conscious of their religious identity and convictions.

By the start of the nineteenth century Friends in the new republic began to go in separate directions. In the towns, religious self-consciousness combined with a desire to begin to relate their religious lives to others around them. These were people whose lives had been changed by the evangelical movement. The Great Awakening had re-emphasized the Divinity of Christ and the importance of His Atonement for sin. It led to the view that the Bible was the work of God, something to be accepted completely, to be taken literally and studied regularly.

The religious reawakening of non-Friends moved them to work on the same social problems in which Friends had been interested. This, in turn, made Friends conscious of the new religious ideas that challenged their traditional views on the Inward Light. The result was that many of these urban, well-educated and sometimes wealthy Friends had been persuaded by the new ideas.

In contrast many traditional Friends living on farms or in small towns devoted themselves to their work and to their religion in traditional ways. They still regarded the Bible as an inspiring book. It followed that Christ was a good man, one wholly attuned to the Inward Light[1]. During the previous century the doctrine of the Inward Light had been given great prominence. During the Quietist period this prominence had led to a neglect of Bible study. Some Friends had even come to regard Bible study as a hindrance to the Inward Light; they saw the Inward Light as sufficient unto itself.

The focus on disownments for disciplinary reasons in the desire for behavioural purity had eclipsed the few disowned for heresy. The focus now shifted from sacrilege to heresy, as belief became more important for Friends. The list of people disowned for heresy in early days had included George Keith and John Perrot. John Wilkinson, John Story and the separatists of Reading and Bristol were disowned more for their actions rather than their beliefs. Hence, their disownment was for sacrilege, rather than heresy. There were other less famous Friends disowned for heresy: Jeffry Bullock was disowned on the 9th day of First month, 1676, for denying Jesus Christ as Savior[2] and John Bartram, as mentioned in the previous chapter, was disowned on the 1st. of Second month, 1758 by Darby Monthly Meeting, Pennsylvania.[3]

John Bartram's heresy was probably not unique for the period. Jack Marietta lists fifteen Friends who were brought to the attention of their monthly meetings for an offense under the category of "theology," of whom twenty percent were disowned, and fifty-four persons under the category of "schism" of whom 28.8 percent were disowned.[4] This would make nineteen who may have committed the offense of heresy. Probably there were others who had avoided attention.

Unlike sacrilege, which is behavior that is defined as offensive to the Divine, heresy is incorrect belief. Behavior is easy to observe, and can be denounced by most believers. Examples for Friends during the eighteenth century included among other things: marrying out, payment of tithes, swearing oaths in court, gambling, and drinking. Wrong belief, which is not easy to observe except in its behavioral consequences, is more difficult to establish and is always taken more seriously. Debate about belief is common, not just among Quakers but within most religions. Incorrect belief that is judged to be heresy requires certain other traits. Lester R. Kurtz has provided a neat summary of these traits:

First, heresy refers to an intense union of both nearness and remoteness. Heretics are within the circle, or within the institution; consequently, they are close enough to be threatening but distant enough to be considered in error... the heretic is a deviant insider...[5]

Second, ... heresy is socially constructed in the midst of social conflict ... The problem of heresy, therefore, is essentially a problem of authority... not every error is heresy ... only that which is held in explicit opposition to ecclesiastical authority...[6]

Third, ... heresy has social consequences as well as social origins ... elites may actually be involved ... in the development of heretical movements ...

Elites do this by redefining the form and substance of a trend and then by driving the adherents of the deviant views together to form a movement to defend themselves from attack.[7]

Friends divisions from the end of the eighteenth century forward show all the characteristics Kurtz summarized, beginning with the division in Ireland.

During the period from before the American Revolution to the War of 1812, spiritual life was low; there was a shortage of Bibles and few Friends read them.[8] Although this says something about American Friends, there is no reason to think that the same thing might not have been said about Irish and English Friends of the same period. The idea is important because it sets the context for the changes that were to take place, changes that were structured by the redefinition of the form and substance of Quakerism by the evangelical elders.

The first serious evidence of a changing state of affairs came in Ireland during the uprising in 1798. Friends in Ireland had managed to establish themselves as truly neutral during the troubles. They had resisted all pressure to take sides. No Irish Friend was disowned for warlike or revolutionary activities. However, some Irish Friends withdrew because they did not accept the literalism of the evangelical elders.

Toward the end of the eighteenth century evangelical Irish Friends wanted every Friend to accept the Bible as the Word of God.[9] Opposition to the elders' biblically based fundamentalist views grew out of Friends reaction to the troubles in Ireland. They had tried to live their lives according to the dictates of the Inward Light and had suffered for it. They found a clear contradiction between the Light they were given and the warring habits of the Israelites in the Bible. Therefore, they objected to the use of the word "Holy" when making reference to "Holy Scripture."

The objection of the dissidents was a combination of two things. The first was Friends' long-standing testimony against warlike activities which combined with the second, the renewed emphasis on Bible study. A careful study of Scripture uncovered knowledge about wars in which God took sides. With the war so close to them and the pressure to take sides so strong, it was more reasonable to reject parts of the Bible than to reject their opposition to war. Opposition to war was traditional among Friends, and their experience with it only made the opposition more powerful. The one thing the idea of the Inward Light does is to make some Friends think matters through very carefully. Inconsistencies in thought get resolved, and such resolution often leads in unexpected directions.

Dissident Irish Friends withdrew because they objected to the uniformity of belief imposed on them. The Friends who remained felt the dissidents should be denied membership for their heresy. The one group of Friends relied on biblical authority, and the dissidents relied on the authority of direct inspiration of the Inward Light. Both sides oversimplified and carried the theological tension to extremes which had been seen earlier in the separations of Perrot and Keith. The theological difference in Ireland was basic to the disagreements which continued to reappear during the entire nineteenth century.

William Savery, who was at Ireland Yearly Meeting in 1798, reports in his journal that in the First month of 1798 he had a conversation with Abraham Shackleton and Robert Greer. These two Irish Friends not only objected to certain parts of the Bible but also rejected the divinity of Christ saying he was " ... a good man ... because he was wholly obedient to this light..."[10] For these two Friends, who were representative of the dissident Irish group, the parts of the Bible that violated their ideals were rejected. This, in turn, led to a rejection of the Bible as "The Word of God." A small number of Irish Friends drew themselves out of the Society over this issue, some in that year and others later. Eventually a few of the dissidents were allowed to return to membership, and others were only allowed to attend meeting for worship.

The small Irish disaffection uncovered differences between two American Friends who visited Irish Yearly Meeting in 1798. One was David Sands, described by Rufus Jones as "... the foremost representative of evangelical views..."[11] Sands felt very strongly that the Friends denial of the Divinity of Christ, the doctrine of the Atonement and the divine inspiration of the Bible were in fundamental error.

The other American Friend was Hannah Barnard. Hannah Barnard, a convinced Friend, was described by Jones as "a woman ... of superior insight and power ... eloquent, impressive and weighty ... [who] commanded respect, and she could hold the attention of large audiences when she spoke."[12] She is seen by Hodgson as a precursor of Elias Hicks and of having developed "a sorrowful unsoundness of principle," and of "doing much mischief in Ireland ..."[13] Yet the mischief and unsoundness of principle followed a period in which she "visited with much satisfaction to Friends generally ... in England, Scotland and Ireland."[14]

Before she traveled to Europe Hannah Barnard was given certificates in "full unity" by her monthly and quarterly meetings. They were endorsed by New York Yearly Meeting. Elias Hicks helped prepare the minute she took with her.[15] At Irish Yearly Meeting she was one of those who was opposed to the elders' evangelicalism, and thereby incurred David Sands' disapproval and concern. Her doubts about the divinely inspired nature of the Bible were not known to those who gave her the certificates to travel. The doubts did not develop and become public until she was in Ireland.

In 1800 Hannah Barnard attended London Yearly Meeting and asked to be liberated to travel to Europe with another Friend. David Sands and Joseph Williams, an Irish Friend, objected. A committee appointed to meet with her did not agree to give her the certificate she wanted. She then appealed successively to the Morning Meeting, the Monthly Meeting of Devonshire House, the Quarterly Meeting and finally again to the yearly meeting held in 1801. The yearly meeting's committee found they could not unite with her view of the Holy Scripture and referred the matter back to her home monthly meeting. On return, her monthly meeting told her to be quiet as a minister, but she persisted in her ministry and was disowned in June, 1802.[16] She later joined the Unitarians.[17] Matters developed in reaction to what must have been fairly widespread agreement with Hannah Barnard's views so that by 1806 both Philadelphia and Baltimore Yearly Meetings were disowning people for questioning the authority of the Scriptures.[18]

The rebellion in Ireland and war in Europe did not stop Friends from traveling. Also, no mention of war in Europe was made at any point in the reports on Hannah Barnard. Therefore, the opposition to Hannah Barnard's travel intentions could only have come from objections to her theological views.

In 1812, Thomas Foster, a London Friend who shared Hannah Barnard's views, was disowned. Others probably shared the same views because in New England, Hodgson describes the " ... wicked and pernicious behavior ... " of some Friends there when he referred to events between 1817 and 1825.[19] These few cases of disownment for heresy, although extremely troublesome, were unimportant when compared to the total number disowned for other causes.

The war of 1812 increased taxes, including those paid in lieu of personal military service in the United States. Like English Friends, those who refused to pay suffered distraint of goods far greater in value than the amount of the tax. Some Friends did weaken and pay the tax. However, at this time there were no disownments for paying the tax or for warlike activities.[20] Once again after the war, Friends renewed their travel in the ministry across the Atlantic. Friends in both Europe and America shared concerns on slavery and prison reform. The combination of travel and shared concerns drew them together.

Knowledge of the ideas of early Friends, even among the well educated, was by now not as strong as it had been. The ideas of the Quietists, based on the sufficiency of the Inward Light, were found wanting when brought into contact with the scholarly, biblically based new evangelicalism. Evangelical ideas therefore gained strength among wealthier Friends, and these ideas were reinforced by the contacts they made in their travels. Wealthy evangelical Friends were likely to be the elders and ministers in the larger centers such as London, Philadelphia and New York. On the other hand, Friends such as Hannah Barnard, who were neither wealthy nor influential and who did not share those ideas, were generally stopped from traveling. The "older" ideas were more likely to be found in the rural areas and among the recent immigrants to the cities.

B. The Explosion

Hannah Barnard and Irish Friends had provided the warning. The real storm centered around a dearly loved old man, Elias Hicks, who devoted himself to his concerns and to the Society of Friends. He was a person later recognized for his outstanding contribution to the abolition of slavery. In many ways he was an unlikely person for the role given him. In 1819, when he was already more than seventy years old, he traveled in the ministry to Philadelphia and preached against the superabundance of wealth he saw there. He strongly emphasized the issues of plainness and simplicity.

In his first public confrontation with the Philadelphia elders he was particularly hard on Friends who used goods produced by slave labor. Prominent among those offended was Jonathan Evans, an elder and sometime clerk of the Philadelphia Yearly Meeting for Sufferings. Evans led a group of men to walk out and force the adjournment of a meeting while Hicks was still speaking. Both men had been offended and were unable to reconcile their differences before parting.[21]

Jonathan Evans was a retired merchant who had dealt in the lumber business. He had served a short time in prison for refusal to serve in the militia and by this time devoted his life to the Society of Friends. He was an elder, clerk of the Meeting for Sufferings and of the yearly meeting's select meeting of ministers and elders. He never spoke during worship but was effective in the business of the Society; he was a man who obviously felt his way was the right way and was willing to use his position to work for his ideals.[22]

A second confrontation between Elias Hicks and Jonathan Evans and other Philadelphia elders in 1822 angered them enormously. After this confrontation Philadelphia did everything they could to discredit Hicks. This confrontation was on the question of who should have the central say in the content of the theology provided to Friends. Evans and the Philadelphia elders did everything they could to retain power on the determination of belief in their hands.[23] Hicks and his supporters were equally clear that the ministers should have the control over what was to be said.

After this confrontation, the Philadelphia elders attacked Hicks' doctrine rather than try to answer his social criticism. They charged him with "holding and promulgating doctrines different from and repugnant to those held by our religious society."[24] In 1823 The Philadelphia Yearly Meeting for Sufferings prepared an official statement of views against Hicks and in reply to the publication of a series of articles in a Baltimore paper entitled the Letters of Paul and Amicus. The Letters were written in the form of a debate between a Presbyterian, Paul, and a Quaker, Amicus. They were written in support of Hicks. The Meeting for Sufferings statement was objected to when it came before the yearly meeting of 1823.[25] It consisted of extracts from a number of approved Quaker authors.

Visiting English Friends reinforced the evangelical ideas of wealthy urban Friends. The visitors' support came again at a crucial point in time — similar in a way to that of their predecessors, the reformers of the election of 1756. There was a curious difference this time around, however. In 1756 persons of wealth and political power were opposed to religious reform. In 1827 the wealthy and powerful within the Society of Friends tried to impose religious reform. In 1827 questions of doctrinal soundness were the public issue; matters of discipline were secondary. Heresy had replaced sacrilege as the issue.

Doctrinal differences were but the surface of a vast chasm between two contending groups. Hicks and other conservative Friends were opposed to the building of canals and railroads. These enterprises were regarded as beneficial by the wealthy Philadelphia Friends merchants. They could afford luxuries that were not available to other Friends. The matter which most deeply disturbed Elias Hicks and the Friends who supported him was the combination of wealth and luxury, and the trading in goods produced by slave labor.[26]

Hicks and his supporters were opposed to the wealthy "Orthodox" on a number of other issues. Hicks supported Friends' schools in opposition to public schools, plainness of dress and household furnishings and separation and the distinctiveness of Friends in the world. They were opposed to the establishment of Bible societies, societies for the propagation of the Gospel (shades of Keith), peace societies and the like.[27] Perhaps the most contentious difference, after the distinct differences in their approach to theology, was the problem of power and control in the Society of Friends. The elders in Baltimore and Philadelphia Yearly Meetings had established formal and informal ways of controlling visiting ministers. They did everything in their power to keep people who disagreed with their evangelical views from traveling in the ministry, or from serving on the committees that made decisions about such ministers.[28] Interestingly, members of Hicks' party were thought of as reformers because of their wish to have Friends return to their ancient practices of plainness and simplicity.[29]

By 1826 the Philadelphia elders and an impressive list of other Friends worked actively against Hicks. The list of his opponents included: David Sands, Thomas Shillitoe, Stephen Grellet, William Forster, Anna Braithwaite, George and Anna Jones, Elizabeth Robson and Isaac Stephenson. So many of them were English evangelicals that it became popular to blame the English for the troubles. Hicks had found great support among other Friends, mainly farmers and journeymen. However, by then there was a fairly general feeling that a division could not be avoided.[30]

There was a confrontation in 1823 between the two contending parties. The "Extracts from the Writings of Primitive Friends" had been prepared by the Meeting of Sufferings. It was presented to the yearly meeting for approval as a definition of Quaker faith. The "Extracts" were rejected by Hicks' supporters as a "creed."[31] The English evangelicals came to the elders defense. In spite of everything the elders could do to stop attacks against them, they lost repeatedly against Hicks' supporters.

Confrontations were almost continuous over the next months. By

56

the close of 1825 H. Larry Ingle describes the point where: "... the two factions within American Quakerdom had almost come to a parting of the ways ..." He says further that "members of practically every monthly meeting had to confront the question about what to do with those ... who disagreed with the dominant faction ..."[32] Relations between the two factions were so bad that minor differences became major, as was the case of a Friend threatened with disownment because he had accused another of being late for meeting, even after an apology had been offered.[33]

Between the yearly meeting held in 1826 and the one in 1827, the evangelicals, especially the English, traveled everywhere they could to persuade Friends. Everywhere they went they faced opposition and complained about "unsound" doctrine. The final confrontation came at Philadelphia Yearly Meeting in 1827. By then both sides were extremely angry with each other, both quite convinced they were right and the other wrong, and both quite willing to do anything to gain their side a victory over the other. The matter that finally brought division was the issue of who should be clerk of the yearly meeting. The Orthodox elders wanted to retain Samuel Bettle, the incumbent clerk. The others, who sided with Elias Hicks, wanted to make John Comly the new clerk. Comly had been the recording clerk. All contentious issues then were referred to the meeting of delegates. Comly's supporters had foreseen the need for support and had sent more than their usual number of delegates. This made Bettle's supporters angry. They felt the meeting had been packed and refused to accept the changes proposed. Normally, when unity was not achieved, the incumbents would remain in their offices. This time, however, the yearly meeting could not agree on this   alternative either.[34]

In an attempt to win the day, Comly's supporters caucused separately one evening to plan their strategy. At this meeting they discussed their withdrawal from the yearly meeting. When the Bettle supporters found this out, there was little hope for a reconciliation. The Comly group, with Elias Hicks present, continued their own meetings between yearly meeting sessions.[35] Comly wrote that the number meeting with him in the Green Street Meeting House increased from about two hundred at the first session to eight hundred at the last.[36] They adjourned their final meeting to meet as a general meeting in June. At the June meeting they agreed to "propose ... the propriety of holding a yearly meeting of Friends in unity" with them.[37] The epistle from the new yearly meeting was dated the 15th to the 19th of Tenth month 1827.

Bettle's supporters blamed Elias Hicks for the separation. They named the new group Hicksites after him, and the name stuck. The Orthodox elders were convinced the separation was based on religious grounds and never recognized the social criticisms leveled against them.

Analysis is complicated by the one-sided record maintained by both London and Philadelphia Yearly Meetings and by the subsequent bias in the historical accounts of the affair. Further distortions came because the movement was named after Elias Hicks. He was but one of the leaders of the movement. What he said was not accepted as a corporate statement by his followers. Robert Doherty made this point when he wrote:

> ... many Friends undoubtedly became Hicksites because they were opposed to Orthodoxy and Orthodox leaders, not because they were drawn to Elias Hicks and his ideas."[38]

After the yearly meeting in April, 1827, both groups traveled widely trying to persuade Friends. The rural Friends who were subjected to Orthodox visits and preaching generally refused to become Orthodox. The Orthodox were not helped by their very critical approach to those who did not agree with them. At the same time the Orthodox, living in the cities and towns, generally remained unaffected by the rural Friends. Each side succeeded in retaining its own members and failed to persuade the others. Although the division had taken place at yearly meeting, most Friends had not been there to take sides. Therefore, it was the travel and preaching after the yearly meeting that forced Friends to take sides. Then, the Friends who had stayed home sided with the people they felt were like them and who had been their representatives at yearly meeting. The urban Friends, were more likely to have been represented by Orthodox Friends and the rural Friends were more likely to feel kindred to John Comly and other supporters of Elias Hicks. In a sense the real division came about after yearly meeting.[39]

After the separation there were court cases over the ownership of property. There were incidents of Friends who worshiped together and then locked each other out of meeting houses when business was to be transacted. There were battles over minute books, and there were cases where Friends used axes to get into meeting-houses. In general, Orthodox Friends were better able to win custody of property because the wealthy were usually the trustees. Hicksites, on the other hand, were able to attract the larger body of members simply because there were more rural than urban Friends.

The data provided by the Hicksites clearly show their majority in Philadelphia Yearly Meeting and in the component quarterly meetings. Orthodox data show, on the contrary, that they outnumbered the Hicksites. The two sets of figures agree fairly closely on the numbers of Orthodox Friends. However, when it comes to the number of Hicksites, the numbers disagree by a factor of three.[40]

The causes of the separation have been analysed and found to be based on a number of theological and economic grounds. William Hodgson lays the blame on the "evil seeds sown so widely over the country ... [that] produced an abundant crop of unsettlement and unbelief, of discord and bitter contention."[41] Clearly the chief villain in his eyes was Elias Hicks. Hicks' "sanctimonious appearance, and profession of being a great reformer, did not perceive the insidious poison which lurked beneath expressions at times designed to cover up the glaring unsoundness of his sentiments."[42] Rufus Jones sees it as an inevitable collision due to "the irresistible maturing of tendencies of thought which at that period were irreconcilable, and could end only in breaking the once united and harmonious body of Friends in two unsympathetic and misunderstanding branches, both shorn of power."[43] Bliss Forbush blamed the English evangelical ministers. Robert Doherty felt that the separation was due to a heterogeneous reaction to orthodoxy that "placed severe strain on all religious organizations, not just the Quakers."[44] Larry Ingle's point of view is that the political and religious differences between the contending parties grew and were exacerbated by ill-considered actions on both sides. The new ideas being introduced by the evangelicals were gradually pushed on all the others until the others either accepted them or withdrew from the Society. The others did not have a clear vision to sustain them. Their old ideals were not enough to oppose social change and emerging ideas, leaving them nothing "save merging with their former opponents."[45]

My own conclusion is that the division was due to a number of factors that came together and built over several years. The earliest disagreements grew out of a reaction to simplistic quietism. The well-educated Friends found their theology had very little content to it when challenged by evangelicalism. Theology was complicated by rural-urban and rich-poor political differences. The increased wealth of urban Quakers, their re-integration into Philadelphia society, and the evangelicalism of visiting English Friends separated them even further from their counterparts. In effect, using Kurtz' idea, the elites were involved in creating the heresy by their acceptance of new ideas.

The Elias Hicks charge in 1819 against the use of and commerce in the goods obtained from the slave trade combined with their faith differences to drive the two groups apart. These very faith differences had divided Friends in Ireland in 1798. Hannah Barnard had brought them with her when she was disowned in 1802 by her monthly meeting. So, by 1819 American Friends had had two decades to grow in different directions.

Between 1819 and 1827 constant debate over religious and social differences further divided the two parties. Aggravating their differences was the attempt by the Orthodox to monopolize power and to use their monopoly to force their evangelical views on the Society. The "reformers," Hicks and his supporters, were not altogether innocent in their attempts to force the Orthodox to change; they simply lacked the power base of the yearly meeting's committee structure. The reformers were in explicit opposition to the authority of the elders, the people who had set themselves up as the ecclesiastical authority. Thus, the second of Kurtz' characteristics was fulfilled. That the reformers were insiders is the obvious first of his characteristics.

The fact that there were two parties that disagreed on several issues is important. The division in 1827 was made possible by the coalescing issues and the growth of contending parties. Thus, although the division fits all three parts of Kurtz' model, he is only referring to the heresy of individuals, not to religious divisions. Large divisions of religious bodies, such as the Religious Society of Friends, come about for additional reasons. One is that there are issues involved that are beyond the questions of heresy. The other is that the heretical movement requires time to develop socially and create the basis for a larger division.

Once the groups had divided, each side followed their social links out to other groups of Friends and, in a sense, forced them to take sides in the disagreement. At this level, the Orthodox were in their weakest position. They did not really understand the conservative nature of their rural counterparts and thus used the wrong approach to win them. So, in the visits to the rural meetings they usually lost the people, even if they retained the property. This filled the year between the meeting in Philadelphia in 1827 and that in New York in 1828.

On a closing note, it should not be forgotten that the Hicksites did not call themselves that, nor did they think of themselves as such. They were Friends who felt they were living in the Light as Friends had always done. Their explanation for the problems was to lay the guilt at the feet of the Philadelphia elders who had exercised tyranny over the yearly meeting. They resented the attacks on Hicks, as they saw him as a valued elder member of the Society. Doherty concludes by writing:

> Those Quakers became Hicksite who were in some way alienated by Orthodox leaders, activities, and beliefs. In this respect, the unity of Hicksites was negative. They agreed on opposition to something, though not clearly defined ..."[46]

Finally, once the court cases were settled, the Hicksites interests were focused on building the meetinghouses and schools they had lost to the Orthodox Friends. They did make a few minor changes in the discipline to avoid having the elders take on too much power in the future.

6

Round Two:
The New York
Division and the Rest

Philadelphia's confrontation in 1827 had come after the close of New York Yearly Meeting. This gave everyone almost a year to prepare for battle. They all recognized New York Yearly Meeting of 1828 would be the important place to justify their actions in Philadelphia. Although Baltimore Yearly Meeting came first, that yearly meeting was largely rural and was not given the importance New York was to receive. Both sides spent the year traveling widely in support of their parties. Fewer Hicksites traveled. However, they had the advantage that Elias Hicks was a member of New York Yearly Meeting.

The Hicksites were angry about the elders' rigid control of Philadelphia Yearly Meeting. The elders were accused of Presbyterianism and Trinitarianism. A meeting of Hicksite representatives was held in October, 1827. It marked the beginning of a separate Philadelphia Yearly Meeting that was to last for a century. They sent out an epistle and appointed delegates to attend New York Yearly Meeting in 1828.

Orthodox Friends had appointed their usual delegates at Philadelphia Yearly Meeting in 1827. They had a clear, simple and self-righteous message: the Hicksites were Deists and Unitarians who had denied their Christianity by withdrawing. Therefore, the separatists were no longer members of the Society of Friends. They should, therefore, be excluded from any form of religious and social intercourse. Hicksites would be allowed to return to the "true" form of Quakerism if they saw the error of their ways and recanted.

Hicks' statements were examined in minute detail. All of his theological faults were ascribed to all who had separated with him. No argument or action by a separatist could be treated as anything but detestable. Orthodox Friends were delighted when:

> Friends came forward and boldly and clearly evinced that they were neither afraid nor ashamed to show themselves on the Lord's side..."[1]

Some other notable traveling English Friends were: George and Anna Jones, Elizabeth Robson and Isaac Stephenson.[2] Thomas Shillitoe was one of the more outspoken English Friends. Because of their active work, blaming the English for the divisions was fairly popular at the time. At least one modern historian, Forbush, has come to do the same.[2]

On "Second Day morning, 26th of Fifth month, 1828" New York Yearly Meeting was gathered. Representatives of both parties were present. Both groups felt morally justified and neither group wanted a compromise. The experience in Philadelphia Yearly Meeting taught the Hicksites an important lesson: that the Friends in possession of the floor of the Yearly Meeting were likely to win the court battles over property. The tactical error in withdrawing was not going to be repeated. Therefore, they determined to force the Orthodox to walk out. When New York Yearly Meeting, 1828, began Thomas Shillitoe was the first to speak:

> I obtained a certificate from my own monthly and quarterly meeting, also from the select Yearly Meeting of Friends held in London, expressive of their concurrence with my traveling in the work of the ministry on this continent, which certificates were read in the last Yearly Meeting of New York, and entered on the records of that Yearly Meeting; as being the case it constitutes me as such a member of it; as such I therefore dare do no other than enter my protest against the meeting's proceeding with its business, whilst so many persons are in the meeting who have no claim or right to sit in this Yearly Meeting.[3]

Hicks replied that he had a right to stay and that he had no objection to continuing the meeting in the presence of Presbyterians. Things then went from bad to worse. After an argument and a struggle for the minute book that destroyed the clerk's table, the Orthodox Friends left. The report from the Orthodox minutes written on the 27th of Fifth month, 1828 describe what happened very nicely:

> The Clerk (i.e. Jonathan Taylor) being absent through indisposition occasioned by injuries in the riot yesterday, the assistant clerk was directed to open the meeting. At the opening of the meeting yesterday a violent and tumultuous assault was made on the meeting by a number of persons who forcibly removed the clerk from the table, inflicting on him serious personal injury, breaking the table to pieces, and committed much violence on the persons of many Friends and so completely interrupting the business of the meeting as to reduce it to the necessity of adjourning, and the rioters still continuing in the house, holding what they called a yearly meeting, and not permitting the representatives and other Friends to assemble there to hold the yearly meeting without interruption, although the demand was made in the name of the trustees and by one of the representatives on behalf of the whole, the meeting, gathered in the yard and after being favored with a solemn season together, adjourned to meet at ten o'clock tomorrow at Short Creek Meeting House.[4] [1828]

The Orthodox women also left the women's meeting. Many left in tears for more than bruised shoulders and broken tables. When it was over, Hicks and Shillitoe took to traveling in the ministry with more determination. Shillitoe followed Hicks in his travels to undo the damage he saw as being done by the older man.

In Indiana the break came between 1827 and 1828.[5] Elisha Bates, who was to influence Friends for a long time, the English evangelicals Isaac and Anna Braithwaite, Ann Jones, the clerk from Ohio Yearly Meeting, Jonathan Taylor and Jeremiah Hubbard, an evangelical from North Carolina, all showed up. On the frontier, Indiana Yearly Meeting was influenced more than others by the denominations living nearby. They remained in the Orthodox fold.

After Indiana Yearly Meeting in 1827 the Meeting for Sufferings produced a twelve page "Testimony and Epistle of Advice" attacking the statements of Elias Hicks and "other similar errors." The "Testimony and Epistle" had quotations from George Fox, William Penn and Robert Barclay. It stressed the importance of the Scriptures and of the Atonement. The Yearly Meeting Minutes of 1827 do not mention the document. Nor do the minutes have a report from the Meeting for Sufferings. The testimony was written afterwards. It probably came in reaction to Anna Braithwaite's visit and to the turmoil they had heard about in Philadelphia. It was signed by Elija Coffin and Rebeka Garretson, clerks.

The "Testimony" was distributed to the subordinate meetings. Immediately it began to cause trouble. Early in 1828 the first division occurred in Blue River Monthly Meeting. The quarterly meeting had

64

tried to lay it down. The claim was that Blue River Friends were "...not capable of transacting the business to honor of Truth..."[6] Blue River refused to be laid down and by mid-year had asked the Orthodox for their share of the property. Miami Quarterly Meeting twice tried and failed to accept the "Testimony." On the second try the Orthodox found themselves to be in the minority and withdrew. They left the meetinghouse in the hands of the Hicksites. After the division, Hicksite Friends wrote about the "Testimony" in the following way:

> Soon after our last Yearly Meeting a Testimony and Epistle of advice from Indiana Yearly Meeting was adopted by our Meeting for Sufferings which together with an address from that Meeting, were urged upon the Quarterly and Monthly Meetings for their observance, accompanied by committees claiming the authority of superior Meetings and identifying a party with themselves; which tended greatly to promote discord and division among us and many valuable members of Society, who could not conscientiously unite with those measures have been, contrary to all right order and Discipline interrupted in their religious rights and privileges. The party assuming the right to govern have laid hold of our Discipline as a sword and wielded it in the will and wisdom of man, thereby departing from our ancient and Christian principles of love, forbearance and charity...[7]

By the end of September, 1828, Indiana Hicksite Friends had organized a new yearly meeting. Elias Hicks was there to encourage them. The avowed purpose of their yearly meeting was to "...restore the unity and harmony of our religious society, and to re-organize our yearly meeting on its ancient foundation and according to our present discipline...[8]"

In summarizing the reasons for the separation in Indiana, Barbara Chase wrote that a doctrinal difference and the question of who wields power were the central issues, as was the case in Ohio. Given the distances from the eastern seaboard and the time it took to travel to Indiana, the reasons for the division are probably the ones Friends had carried there with them. One should add that they had not spent enough time together to find reasons to stay together. Also the Indiana Friends, who were isolated from other rural Friends, lived in close proximity to non-Friends. The religious views of the non-Friends were important in providing them with a viewpoint that was sympathetic to the Orthodox party.[9]

All the yearly meetings in North America went through some trauma that year. In Baltimore Yearly Meeting more than two thirds joined the Hicksites. Virginia and North Carolina did not divide and only a small group withdrew in New England. They, along with London and Dublin, aligned themselves with the Orthodox and refused to correspond with the separatists, now labeled Hicksites.[10]

In Ohio Yearly Meeting the final division came on a wet, rainy morning. Thomas Shillitoe, the English Friend, wrote:

> Printed notices had been served on E. Hicks and others, and copies nailed on the doors of the men's and women's house, signed by the trustees of the property, warning them not to enter the meeting-house during the sittings of the Yearly Meeting; the numerous door-keepers were also in attendance, but the separatists became so violent it appeared no longer possible for the door-keepers to maintain their posts, ... the mob poured into the house...[11]

Short tempers were the order of the day. A board cracked in the gallery and in the panic, one man jumped out of the window. The clerk, Jonathan Taylor, was attacked and got his glasses broken. The recording clerk's table was destroyed and one man was bitten. The focus of the final bout was, again, the identity of the clerk. Each side tried to get its own representative in that position. About two thirds became Hicksites there. However, in a curiously different approach there was no conflict over the yearly meeting property. Because the Hicksites set their yearly meeting at a different time of year, they avoided a court battle over the yearly meeting property. The Mt. Pleasant Meeting House was eventually to be shared by three Ohio Yearly Meetings.

Orthodox Friends disowned the Hicksites in all yearly meetings as soon as they were discovered. Orthodoxy of belief was now required. They rejected the openness that had been a part of the belief in the Inward Light. Hicksites were not burned at the stake. However, some of the Orthodox may have liked to do so. Hicksites were seen as inspired by "the Antichrist." Reports damning them were circulated. Descriptions of events shocked people all over. London led the way and refused to receive their epistles, and the others followed suit. This left a large part of the Society of Friends in isolation for many years.[12] After a time, sorrow replaced bitterness and anger. It was a sorrow over the loss of contact with friends. The Orthodox would have liked the Hicksites to apologize, recant and offer to return. If they could not bring themselves to do this, they should have the grace to simply vanish as a body.

On the other side, the Hicksites were quite convinced they were right. The Orthodox had violated the Discipline and claimed power for themselves. Therefore, the Orthodox should be the ones to apologize and ask to be allowed to return. Being open to the much more flexible guidings of the Inward Light, Hicksite Friends were more open to reunion. They were also much less likely to disown people than were the Orthodox.

Once the divisions were complete both parties published their versions of what had taken place. Friends history and beliefs were reinterpreted by both sides. The Orthodox produced a book edited by Thomas Evans that went through a number of editions. The first edition was issued with the approval of Philadelphia Meeting for Sufferings on the 19th of Tenth month, 1827. Approval for its publication was signed by Jonathan Evans, clerk, the person who had the run-in with Elias Hicks over the matter of use of slave products in 1819.

The book, *An Exposition of the Faith of the Religious Society of Friends, Commonly called Quakers, in the Fundamental Doctrines of the Christian Religion; Principally Selected from their early Writings*, set out to prove that the theological stand of the Orthodox was supported by statements of early Friends. As early Friends had said and published a great deal, they were able to find ample support. Items chosen to be included came from letters, pamphlets and books—principally Barclay's *Apology*—, the very things written in defense of Friends early ideas. Each side tried to prove their views to be sound, but it was the Orthodox who tried to prove the other side was unsound. In many ways the collections produced by Evans are attempts to establish the continuity of belief with early Friends. Evans' action and the minutes written by both sides is part of what has been called "remaking the symbolic forms of the belief system." Evans selected material that fit his particular beliefs. He neglected the matters that would have supported Hicks. He was, then, rewriting history by selective editing.

The Hicksites did not have the same drive to prove they were theologically right. The quotations they used were from the same sources, but they did not quote the same things. The Orthodox were out to prove their evangelical views were closer to the original forms of Quakerism than the views expressed by Elias Hicks. The Hicksites, in contrast, did not feel they had to justify their stand on the Inward Light, as this was available to all who sought it. Their argument was on a totally different level. It was basically a complaint about the authoritarian nature of the Orthodox elders:

> ...We believe measures have been pursued by one part of society assuming the right of government in the Church, inconsistent with

right order and discipline which have proved oppressive and tended to deprive many of our Religious and Civil rights and privileges, and thereby interrupted that badge of Christian fellowship and bond of Religious union which have hitherto bound our Religious society together ...[14]

Their differences could now be accommodated in a relatively small meeting. In today's terms Thomas Evans' viewpoint was not very far from John Comly's. Elias Hicks was puzzled by the violence of the controversy over "a little difference of opinion on abstract subjects."[15]

In spite of their isolation, the Hicksites continued to go to worship, live by their principles, send out epistles and carry on as they always had done. When the epistles went unanswered they simply stopped sending them. Visits and travel in the ministry were also attempted with Orthodox meetings. These efforts became sporadic when they were only accidentally successful. So, Hicksite Friends devoted themselves to their concerns and to rebuilding their meetings and schools. Like Orthodox Friends, they, too, did their share of re-writing history. On the frontier, Hicksite Friends blamed the separation on Eastern Friends. They used this to explain the reorganization of the meetings in Western New York State and Upper Canada. Scipio Quarterly Meeting, Canada Half Yearly Meeting and Pelham Half Yearly Meeting came together to form Gennessee Yearly Meeting.

Legal battles to decide ownership of meetinghouses and schools were similar to those seen in the Wilkinson-Story separation. There were similar encounters over minute books; Friends were locked out of "their" meeting houses; and, some forced their way in despite the locks. Simultaneous meetings were held in the same place with different clerks. In some cases in spite of their differences, they were able to continue meeting for worship together.

In most cases except in Pennsylvania and New Jersey the courts gave the property to the larger body. When judgment was given for the Hicksites, they were more likely to compensate the Orthodox for their share of the property. In Pennsylvania and New Jersey Hicksite Friends had already started to build new meetinghouses and schools by the time of the yearly meeting in New York in 1828.

7

The Beaconite
Separation
in England

In England Friends looked with horror at the American conflict. At the same time, however, they had problems of their own. When the wars with Napoleon were over, Britain went through the turmoil of adjusting to peace. The most pressing problems were a drop in the price of wheat and massive unemployment. To solve the first, politically powerful landlords were able to get help in the form of laws controlling the importation of wheat. This pushed up the price of bread for people who had been released from work in the arms industries and from the armed forces. Naturally, there was a strong reaction. The frustration led to violence which produced repression. The most violent event took place at St. Peter's Fields on August 16, 1819. Then in 1833 slavery was abolished. In 1835 municipal reform also took place. These were two of the many changes Friends had worked for.

During the first half of the nineteenth century the Society of Friends in Great Britain gradually lost members. Their numbers declined from about 19,800 at the beginning of century to about 14,300 in 1851. Most of the loss came as a result of withdrawals and disownments. However, about three hundred of the 5,500 member loss came from the Beaconite separation brought about by Isaac Crewdson's actions in Manchester in 1836.[1] The number lost in this separation was tiny when compared to the Hicksite separation. It was smaller even than the number of Friends disowned for revolutionary activity by Philadelphia Yearly Meeting. However, this small separation is the largest that has taken place in Britain since the Wilkinson-Story separations of the seventeenth century.

The Beaconite Separation grew out of the opposition in London Yearly Meeting to the ideas of Elias Hicks. Hicks' dangerous views had been ascribed to all the people who had withdrawn with him. "Hicksism" was, therefore, to be isolated at all costs, almost as if it were smallpox. Friends from the separating yearly meetings were given no official recognition when they visited or traveled in the ministry. London Yearly Meeting Friends did not read Hicksite Epistles or send them the ones produced in London. Criticism and unfortunate reports about the separatists were accepted completely. Nobody bothered to ask Hicks' partisans what their views were on his ideas. Instead, all that had gone wrong was blamed on the "evil" influence and inadequate spiritual insight of the Hicksite ministers. English Friends had looked for and found explanations for the violent and un-Quakerly behavior. At the same time, they did not hear the criticisms leveled at the Orthodox. The Hicksites' social message was totally lost.

Isaac Crewdson, who became the focus of the controversy, was a strong-minded and relatively wealthy textile merchant used to having his own way. The conflict began in 1835 when Crewdson wrote and published *A Beacon to the Society of Friends*. It was a total rejection of Hicks and of the idea of the Inward Light. Crewdson's ideas were quite similar to the ones held by other evangelical Friends. It was, therefore, much to his surprise that it produced a strong negative reaction. He was only writing widely shared convictions in attacking something many Friends felt was dangerous. He wrote:

> The Great deception appears to have originated in the assumption, that we are authorized to expect to be taught the true knowledge of God and His salvation—our duty to him, and our fellow-men, immediately by the SPIRIT, independently of his revelation through the Scriptures,—an assumption which is unsupported by the Scriptures, contradicted by fact and one which renders its votaries a prey to many fatal delusions...2

The *Beacon* brought replies and started an angry debate. London Yearly Meeting appointed a committee to visit Manchester to resolve the disagreement. The committee, which included Joseph John Gurney, recommended that the monthly meeting not proceed against Crewdson for "doctrinal unsoundness." Crewdson was told to keep silent in the meeting for worship. He was not to sit on the meeting of ministers and elders. He objected to this treatment and resigned.

70

Fifty-two other members resigned with him. The immediate withdrawal was limited to Crewdson's friends and their relatives. They included a former yearly meeting clerk, John Wilkinson, Luke Howard, prominent in his own right and one who had been involved in the problems with Hannah Barnard, and several members of the Braithwaite family. The people lost to Friends included the children who had been given birthright membership.[3]

Discussion on the Beacon was heated and sometimes bitter. Friends were deeply upset, as their loss was such a personal one. A sense of the depth of feeling is given many years later by Joseph Bevan Braithwaite when he wrote:

> ...the influence of the controversy was wide-spread owing largely to family connections among Friends at Kendal and Manchester and a few at Birmingham ... Largely as a result of this controversy my beloved brother Isaac and my sister Anna were thrown under the influence of the late Baptist Noel and my dear brother Robert became a clergy-man, and my brother Foster and my sister Caroline [Joseph Bevan's twin] also withdrew from the Society leaving my brother Charles and myself the only members of the family who remained Friends. All this was a great trial to my dear father and mother.[4]

The matter was obviously hurtful to Bevan Braithwaite. Later on he is reported to have refused to discuss new religious ideas as he had made up his mind on the matter many years earlier. And, although he was involved in mediating in the separation of the Manchester rationalists in the 1860s, he makes no mention of them or of the Fritchley group.

After the division Crewdson's group built their own chapel and began a new periodical, *The Inquirer*. They made a concerted effort to organize themselves on Biblical grounds. After searching through the New Testament, which gave them little help, they decided to appoint deacons and elders. They drafted a statement of faith, rejected birthright membership and the ministry of women. They also began baptizing, singing hymns and taking the Lord's Supper. The group's final decline came after Crewdson died in 1844. The chapel they had built to seat six hundred was sold to the Baptists.[5]

Isolation from the separatists in North America had left English Friends without having to face the duality of their faith. Crewdson, by his actions, forced them to examine it. Fortunately, Sarah Grubb and Joseph John Gurney were both determined that Friends should not divide over their theological disagreements. Sarah Grubb was a

Quietist with a strong belief in the Inward Light. Joseph John Gurney was strongly evangelical. The line then came to be drawn between Crewdson and other evangelical Friends over whether the conservative Friends could be tolerated.

After the withdrawal London Yearly Meeting in 1836 discussed the place and authority of the Bible for Friends. Its centrality and importance to the discussion was now obvious. The General Epistle from that year reads in part as follows:

> It has ever been, and still is, the belief of the Society of Friends, that the Holy Scripture of the Old and New Testament were given by inspiration of God; that therefore the declarations contained in them rest on the authority of God Himself and there can be no appeal from them to any authority whatsoever; that they are able to make us wise unto salvation through faith which is in Christ Jesus; being the appointed means of making known to us the blessed truths of Christianity; that they are the only divinely authorized record of the doctrines which we are bound as Christians to believe, and of the moral principles which are to regulate our actions; that no doctrine which is not contained in them can be required of any one to be believed as an article of faith; that whatsoever any man says or does which is contrary to scriptures, though under profession of immediate guidance of the Spirit, must be reckoned and accounted as mere delusion.[6]

Although in this statement Friends did not reject personal revelation, they did require that any such be tested against the Scriptures. At the same time London Yearly Meeting did not insist on a declaration of faith from members. The effects of the statement were to limit discussion and force Friends into a common mold. The epistle was very similar to the statement of faith required by Crewdson's group.

The Hicksite separation did not have the effect one might have predicted on London Yearly Meeting. Reports of extreme radicalism and sole reliance on the Inward Light brought a rejection of that doctrine. As many still felt the doctrine of the Inward Light was central to Friends beliefs, its total rejection was too extreme. Crewdson's rigidity on this point led to a reaction that made him withdraw with his supporters. Unlike Philadelphia, in London the theological issue did not divide the wealthy from the non-wealthy. Instead it created a division within the economic and social elite.

Another reason London Yearly Meeting did not divide is due to the efforts of those involved in handling the *Beacon* affair. Joseph Bevan

Braithwaite has been referred to above, but he was a very young man at the time. Towering above him and the others is Joseph John Gurney. Gurney shared many of the views espoused by Crewdson. In contrast, however, Gurney developed a strong regard for the "perceptible guidance of the Spirit." The conservatives also felt something important would be lost if they did not stay together. As a result London Yearly Meeting was enabled to produce the Epistle for that year. Much of the credit is due to Friends determination to hang together. They were also helped by the nature of the social context of the Society of Friends in England at that time.

In England, Friends were a social unit in a way the American Friends simply were not. The early practice of apprenticing young Friends to older ones had moved most of them into the industrial cities. They were often employed by Friends there. Obvious distinctions between rural and urban, poor and wealthy Friends such as existed in America were blurred by their regular contact. They worshiped together and worked together on their concerns. Although there were differences in wealth, when Friends in Britain examined their theological differences they did it with people of their own meetings whom they knew well. Discussions on important questions were carried on at yearly meeting with people also who knew each other as friends. Discussions were not carried on with comparative strangers whom people saw infrequently, as in the American yearly meetings.

Sara Grubb and Joseph John Gurney were the English equivalent of a Hicksite and an Orthodox. They tangled sharply in 1836 and 1837 over Gurney's request for a traveling minute for his American trip. However, they knew each other and respected each other. This allowed them to accept their differences without bringing on a division. In Philadelphia the opposing factions had only met in acrimony. Perhaps the most obvious thing in all the pain is that when affection, forbearance and regard are present, astonishingly different groups can remain together.

The social differences between London Yearly Meeting and the American yearly meetings explain the different consequences of disagreement. In America a large proportion of people were isolated from the rest for over a century. In England only one monthly meeting was divided. The yearly meetings on both sides of the Atlantic had both been exercised by the Hannah Barnard, David Sands debate. Therefore, they had about as long to disagree on the same theological issues.

Philadelphia Yearly Meeting was composed of two sets of very different Friends. The urban, wealthy and the tradesmen and cash-crop farmers with links to the city on one side. They faced the large bulk of subsistence farmers and recent migrants to the city. The two sides had different views on many issues. The Orthodox tried to force change on to the others. The others complained about the tight control of the yearly meeting. Hicks' social criticism was never answered, which exacerbated the social divisions that were there.

Sarah Grubb and Joseph John Gurney knew each other and worked together, even though they disagreed in very fundamental ways. Gurney did not try to exclude Grubb from influence in the activities of the yearly meeting. He made no attempt like Jonathan Evans' to control membership of the meetings of elders and the yearly meeting clerk.

The division in Philadelphia was, therefore, a combination of deep theological differences with political and social discord. Ideals on both sides were violated. Finally, the the exclusion of the Hicksites from participation in the meetings of elders made things worse. None of these factors were at play in England.

In England the theological differences worked themselves out on a background that was quite different. Mutual respect and consideration were a large part of it. In Manchester it was one group in one meeting that left. Albeit, they were a group that was very important in the life of the yearly meeting. Their social links to other groups in the country were strong. Hence, the hurt that was caused when the break came. However, the context of political, social, personal and internal power struggle was missing. Also missing was the deep dislike the protagonists had for each other in Philadelphia. Hence, although very important in its effect on London Yearly Meeting, the Beaconite Division did not have the large and long-term consequences it had in Philadelphia.

8

The Anit-Slavery Separation

In one of his lectures Rufus Jones is reported to have said:

> ... The Society of Friends has always tended to produce two distinct
> types ... on the one hand, a small body of individuals unreservedly
> committed to the ideal ... on the other, a somewhat larger number
> 'who have held it to be equally imperative to work out their prin-
> ciples of life in the complex affairs of the community and the state,
> where to gain an end one must yield something ... where to achieve
> ultimate triumph one must risk his ideals to the tender mercies of
> a world not yet ripe for them.[1]

After the 1828 divisions, questions about the Inward Light were no
longer debated. Each of the two separating groups tried to retain as
much control over their own people as they could. The Hicksite
camp was not bothered by the isolation of the poorer and more rural
majorities after the court cases were settled. The West was opening,
and Friends, like so many others, were moving. They had opened
western Pennsylvania and were moving into Ohio and Indiana by the
time of the 1827-8 conflict.

In both Ohio and Indiana, the Society of Friends had been split in
two. In Ohio the two groups of Friends shared the building used for
yearly meeting gatherings for a number of years. They decided to do
this instead of paying the other group "an equivalent for their
relinquishment, of their right to their part agreeably to the numbers
of their relative parties ..." The Orthodox party had retained the

minute books, so Hicksites had to begin with a new set. They had chosen David Willis and Lydia Hoag as their clerks.[2]

By 1830 the fractioned Society of Friends in America was composed of eight Orthodox yearly meetings (Philadelphia, New York, Baltimore, Ohio, Indiana, New England,North Carolina and Virginia) and six Hicksite yearly meetings (Philadelphia, New York, Baltimore, Ohio, Indiana and a very small group in New England). In the next decade there were a few changes in the Hicksite groups. New England Friends joined New York Yearly Meeting and New York set off its western and northern portion as Genessee Yearly Meeting in 1834. The Wilbur-Gurney division was still to come.

A. Orthodox Disunity

Just when religious matters had settled down for Friends on the frontier, they became involved again in a division. It happened in Indiana, then the largest yearly meeting in the world.[3] Friends had been opposed publicly to slavery from the time of George Keith. In most cases they had been free from holding slaves for many decades. The ones who still owned slaves were those who had found no way to release their slaves without injury to the slaves. Yet, the issue of slavery became the focus of acrimony and a separation in Indiana Yearly Meeting. This was in spite of the ancient testimonies, the lack of slaves, and the work on behalf of slaves.

The view we have of slavery today makes understanding pre-Civil War problems difficult. It is now abhorrent to hold someone else as a form of property. It is hard to understand why a Christian with a moral conscience at all could do other than oppose it. Yet, the majority of the Christian groups living in the South found sufficient biblical authority to oppose the efforts of the abolitionists. Nowhere, for example, is slavery forbidden in the Bible. The theme there is one of telling servants to be obedient and respectful to their masters (see: Ephesians 6: 5-8 and Titus 2:9).[4]

Our view of slavery is affected by the arguments that helped bring slavery to an end. It is complicated by the exaggerations and bitterness that led to a civil war. Post-war statements created a picture of the South and of slavery that would have been different had slavery quietly withered away without a war. Before the Civil War slavery was seen by many as a benign condition that helped promote economic prosperity. Only after 1830 did a large proportion of the public come to see slavery as the most immoral and damaging thing ever done to human beings. It was at this time the people opposed to slavery became radical and willing to risk violence.

As the question of slavery became politicized, some Friends began to find allies in their fight against this evil. The conflict was most severe for Friends in the South. Legislation in the South made it hard to free slaves and just as hard for freed slaves to remain free. Therefore, many southern Friends moved to Indiana and Ohio taking their slaves along. Once there they provided their ex-slaves with the necessities to live as free people. The number of Friends migrating from the South became so high that Virginia Yearly Meeting was almost depleted. It chose to become a part of Baltimore Yearly Meeting in 1843. When Friends began to move west, they were a minority among the many opposing slavery. Friends views, like those of others, were affected by the experience and information available to them. It was this group of former Southerners who had first-hand experience with the institution of slavery who formed the core of the radical anti-slavery movement among Friends. Friends who had little or no contact with slavery were more willing to take the slower route to change.

At the time there were two basic approaches to the abolition of slavery among Friends. One recognized the property value of slaves as very important to slave owners. These Friends hoped people would grow out of their need for slaves. They found places in Africa for the return of ex-slaves and tried to get the slave-holding laws changed. Individual Friends had tried to help by purchasing and freeing a number of slaves at enormous cost to themselves.

A radical approach was taken by other Friends. Some, in their abhorrence of the practice, had allied themselves with non-Friends to do everything they could to overcome slavery. In the process Hicksite and Orthodox bodies were faced with a dilemma. The Fugitive Slave Act made it illegal to help runaway slaves. Pro-slavery advocates saw the work of anti-slavery bodies as a form of theft. Radical Friends were, to them, committing illegal acts that were provoking strong reactions. In the ensuing riots, a Friend's printing house was destroyed. The violence and illegality of the anti-slavery groups was more than conservative Friends could bear, especially when Friends names were linked to the violence.

In Ohio and Indiana many Friends had actively worked to free slaves and were deeply involved in the Underground Railroad. Disagreeing with them were people who had not been touched personally by slavery. Some of these people were merchants who had not yet freed themselves from dealing in the products of slavery. The two sides were agreed only that slavery was wrong. There were no theological issues involved. The matter of wealth was seldom mentioned. They disagreed on the form and vigor of opposition to slavery and on the urgency of the problem.

Indiana Yearly Meeting held third of Tenth month, 1839, reported: "Our testimony against slavery was also brought afresh to the view of Friends with affectionate desires that it may be faithfully maintained."[5] Their testimony on slavery was published in 1839 in The Discipline of the Society of Friends of Indiana Yearly Meeting and was quite clear:

> As a religious society, we have found it to be our indispensable duty to declare to the world, our belief of the repugnancy of slavery to the christian religion. It therefore remains to be our continued concern to prohibit our members from holding in bondage our fellow men. And, at the present time, we apprehend it to be incumbent on every individual deeply to consider his own particular share in this testimony...

Friends were quite consistent in this regard. For example, the report of the "Committee on the Concerns of the People of Color" read in part: "We desire in brotherly love to remind such that our testimony against slavery is purely a religious ceremony."[6]

In the three years between 1839 and 1842 the disagreement over tactics reached the Meeting for Sufferings. The Meeting for Sufferings was dominated by a group of conservatives opposed to radical tactics. In the absence of radical Friends the conservatives disqualified eight members of the Meeting for Sufferings from serving on yearly meeting committees. Further, no person "opposed to the advice and travail of the body" was to be allowed a position of responsibility on any committee or anywhere else in the yearly meeting. To make certain this policy was followed they insisted that all nominations have the approval of the elders before submission to the clerk. Some of the people disqualified were elderly Friends who had long held important positions within the yearly meeting.

Anti-slavery Friends in Indiana were outraged by this action. They argued against the abuse of power by some of the elders but lost the day. In their frustration they proposed having those sharing their view remain behind at the rise of the yearly meeting for a conference on the matter. When refused access to the yearly meetinghouse rooms, they were forced to go elsewhere. They met in Newport in January, 1843, to reorganize Indiana Yearly Meeting on the basis of "true principles."[7]

When news of the separation reached London Yearly Meeting, they were moved to send some Friends to attempt a reconciliation. The English Friends carried with them a letter from London Yearly Meeting which read in part:

> ... Accept, we beseech you, our earnest and affectionate entreaty that you will relinquish your separate Meetings for this purpose — will wholly discontinue them and again assemble for the public worship of Almighty God with those with whom you have been accustomed to meet.[8]

The delegation that carried the letter to Anti-Slavery Friends felt their duty was simply to exhort the separatists to return to the fold. Charles Osborn, Henry W. Way, Eliza Coffin, Levi Coffin, Benjamin Stanton, Jacob Grave, William Locke and others were in no mind to "relinquish their separate meetings." By then nobody was willing to listen to the other side.

In fairness to the English Friends, it should be clarified that there were a series of strong letters published in the British *Friend* during this period that were quite clear in their support for the separatists. One letter written by Joseph Sturge reads in part:

> ... The value of the caution against joining "political Abolitionists," may be estimated by English Friends, when informed, that our Society in America, with a few rare exceptions, participate in the national feeling, that to take part in politics is the duty of every citizen; and an American correspondent of mine, who was well assured of its truth, states "that it was a fact no less melancholy than true, that of all religious bodies, none went in such unbroken phalanx to vote of Tyler, the Slave Holder as the Society of Friends." ...[9]

No other Orthodox yearly meetings divided on this issue, even though they disagreed noisily. T. E. Drake's summary of the effects of the separation was that it:

> ... cleared the air like a thunderstorm. By precipitating the radicals out ... the schism relieved the tension ... the Quaker majority — Orthodox and Hicksite — decided finally that their religious Society must follow a quiet way in opposing slavery."[10]

A lot happened in the next few years. The Oregon crisis with its battle cry : "Fifty-four Forty or Fight" suggested an impending war with Canada. It was averted by the war with Mexico over Texas, New Mexico and California. The war was enmeshed politically with the anti-slavery issue. The outcome was a national debate over whether the newly acquired lands should be open to slavery. A national compromise reached in 1850 defined which states should be free. In the struggle for compromise, a large part of the territory acquired was defined as free, but at the same time the Fugitive Slave Act was strengthened. It now became a criminal offense to help free a slave. Escaping slaves were open to recapture and return for a bounty. The ferocity of the Fugitive Slave Act rapidly changed the views of most Friends who had driven out the anti-slavery group only a few years before. Public opinion changed and the pro-slavery groups outside the South lost much of their moral legitimacy. Polarization on slavery caused the Baptist, Methodist and Presbyterian churches to split into northern and southern branches, some dividing again into White and Black sub-branches. Friends did not divide in this fashion. Instead the once conservative majority of Friends in Indiana took on a position very similar to that originally held by the anti-slavery minority.

By 1852 there was a definite agreement that the Anti Slavery Friends would be accepted back with no apology on either side. Those most hurt by the separation eventually died, and the rest quietly rejoined the majority or moved into other churches. Had Friends differed on more than how to oppose slavery there might now be northern and southern branches of the Society of Friends. However, thanks to the historical stand on the matter of slavery, this separation very quickly became history.

B. Disunity among the Hicksites

Hicksite Friends faced divisions between abolitionists and others in Ohio, Michigan, Illinois, Indiana, New York and Pennsylvania in the period after 1843. Orthodox and Hicksite Friends had worked together for years in the radical anti-slavery bodies. The divisions in 1827-28 did not break the continuity of their work. This helps account in part for the ability of Ohio Friends of different persuasions to share their yearly meeting premises. Unlike the large separation over the issue of slavery in Indiana Yearly Meeting (O) the Hicksites went through a series of small scale withdrawals. The division in Indiana only served to bring the matter forcibly to everyone's attention.

The first sign of irreconcilable difference appeared in Green Plains Monthly Meeting in 1843 and 1844. They and other Hicksite Friends in western Ohio formed a new yearly meeting in 1849. They called themselves the Green Plains Yearly Meeting to distinguish themselves from the rest of the members of Indiana Yearly Meeting (H). There were similar differences in Ohio Yearly Meeting (H). This created another division in New Garden Quarter that spread to Salem Quarter. This division led to the formation of Ohio Yearly Meeting of Friends of Human Progress in 1856.[11]

The anti-slavery division among Ohio Hicksites freed the radicals and allowed them to go on making other changes. By 1850 the Green Plains group was referring to itself as the "Friends who have Adopted the Congregational Order of Church Government." They received "an address from the Yearly Meeting of Congregational Friends held at Waterloo, New York on the 6th. month of 1850." Concerns of the Ohio meetings were about the subservient position of women, slavery, land monopoly and capital punishment. They sent epistles to their Michigan and New York counterparts, the Ohio Yearly Meeting (H) and to Anti-slavery Friends in Indiana. These echoed the statements and concerns of the New York group which, like the one in Michigan, had separated from its parent meeting in 1849.

When Congregational and Progressive Friends separated from their Hicksite yearly meetings, their statements often echoed the statements that had led to the original separations. Younger and more radical Friends were dissatisfied with the oppressive behavior of the meetings of ministers and elders. They were also quite unhappy with the rigidity of the beliefs held by elders. Slavery was not the only issue in these new separations. Radical Friends, numbering Lucretia Mott among them, had allied themselves with others to fight for many things. Abolition was but one of the issues. Yet, as this issue became more political and was illegal, older Friends were greatly disturbed. They feared compromise of Friends principles. Accordingly, they tried to control the radicals by using the Discipline. When the matter came to a head, the radicals withdrew to set up their own meetings.

The main principles of the separating progressive Friends listed by Allen Thomas were:

> ... (1) Freedom of belief or liberty of conscience; (2) absolute individual freedom of speech and action as far as practicable; (3) Congregational meetings with freedom of action in each meeting; (4) Annual meetings with advisory powers only; (5) All meetings open to interested persons whether members or not; (6) No recording of Ministers, and the abolition of Meetings of Ministers and Elders; (7) Whole-hearted support of the Anti-Slavery cause and of the Abolitionists; (8) Absolute equality of the sexes, including suffrage; (9) Refraining from the manufacture, sale and use of intoxicating liquors as a beverage; (10) General reformation

At least eight new yearly meetings were created by the separations in Hicksite meetings between 1848 and 1857. After the Civil War, Progressive Friends slowly disappeared. Their main reason for being was their fight against slavery. Once that question was resolved, their main reason for being went with it. The majority of Progressive Friends found their ways into other religious groups. The largest number of them became Unitarians. The one meeting that continued beyond 1865 was reported to have been still meeting as late as 1920. It had become only a philanthropic discussion group by then and no longer held to Friends principles or practices.[13]

9

Traditionalism, Idealism and Modernity; Wilbur vs. Gurney

The second series of large divisions among American Quakers in the nineteenth century began in 1845 in New England, the largest yearly meeting not divided by the earlier Orthodox/Hicksite troubles. Two people, Joseph John Gurney and John Wilbur, a New England elder, served as the main protagonists. Their names have been joined to identify it as the Gurneyite/Wilburite separation. Both Gurney and Wilbur were birthright Friends. Both were well known to Friends in England and America. Both were well regarded ministers who had devoted much of their lives to the Society of Friends. Both were deeply concerned for the Religious Society of Friends, and both wanted the best that could be given for it.

New England Yearly Meeting was made immune to the Orthodox/ Hicksite separation by an even earlier series of events, one which involved John Wilbur between 1816 to 1824. During these earlier events the issues in New England were similar to the ones which later divided Philadelphia. Charges were made by elders and ministers that people were suffering from a "spirit of delusion." They were people who had been affected by The New-Light movement. Their major offense was rooted in their belief in the primacy and sufficiency of the Inward Light. They rejected the Bible as a source of authority treating the historical books of the Old Testament as pure allegory. Their beliefs came out in shared messages in meeting for worship that were unacceptable to the elders. The elders, in turn, were accused of "dead formality" and the meetings were derided for being "priest and elder-ridden."[1]

In an effort to overcome the rigid formality of their meetings, some younger members in Lynn, Massachusetts, had sat in the ministers' gallery and had been ejected. One of them, Benjamin Shaw, then tried a second time and was physically thrown out of the meeting house. One of his partisans, John Alley, Jr., took this as a declaration of war. He decided to go into meeting armed with a sword to defend himself. He had to be disarmed, and was charged and imprisoned for rioting.[2] They and the group that supported them were then disowned, creating long lasting ill feelings.

At New Bedford, Massachusetts, the elders were just as rigid and formal. They refused younger people the right to sit in the gallery or to have a say in their meetings. When dissension appeared, the charge, as in Lynn, was that they had ideas that were unacceptable to the ministers and elders. John Wilbur was a member of the investigating committee sent by the Quarterly Meeting to New Bedford. In New Bedford, however, the focus of dissension was on two middle-aged and wealthy sisters, Elizabeth Rodman and Mary Ritch. Both were members of the "Select Meeting." It took longer for matters to come to a head in New Bedford than it had in Lynn, because important members were involved. However, Elizabeth Rodman and Mary Ritch were disowned after visits from an investigating committee. Public meetings were held in Lynn in their support.[3]

Elizabeth Rodman and Mary Ritch had been accused of exalting the Inward Light over the Scriptures. All the dissidents felt freed by their reliance on the primacy and sufficiency of the Inward Light. This had freed them from reliance on either the Scriptures or the discipline of the group. They denied the divinity of Jesus Christ and the efficacy of His Atonement. The differences between the elders and Elizabeth Rodman, Mary Ritch and their supporters was very similar to the theological differences that had divided Ireland Yearly Meeting. The same differences caused Hannah Barnard's disownment and are the ones which were to divide Orthodox from Hicksite. Ill feeling lasted in New Bedford for years. In 1829 when Mary Newhall, one of the dissidents, died, she was buried in the Friends burial ground but only after the elders had carefully built a fence around her grave to keep her apart. The elders wanted to quarantine the dissidents even after death.[4]

Perhaps John Wilbur was reminded of the New Bedford incident when he visited England and Ireland several years later in 1831-33.

There he was faced with the strong reaction to Quaker conservatism in all its forms. He was frustrated by the new Quaker evangelicalism he found there. He was encouraged, however, to find many who agreed with him. On his return, Wilbur wrote and published "Letters to a Friend on Some of the Primitive Doctrines of Christianity." The letters were written to George Crossfield and were published in The British Friend. Later they were republished in Wilbur's *Journal.* John Wilbur's visit to England produced an obsession for him of the dangers of Joseph John Gurney's teaching. After 1832, Wilbur never recognized Gurney's acceptance of the "immediate guidance of the Spirit".[5]

Joseph John Gurney's visit to the United States in 1837-1840 made John Wilbur very uncomfortable. Gurney traveled with a certificate from London Yearly Meeting. It had been given him reluctantly. The English Friends who opposed his travels in the ministry were the same ones who had received " ... great satisfaction ... " from Wilbur's visit. They included Sarah Grubb, who opposed Gurney's visit. She did not unite in providing Gurney with his traveling minute. Wilbur knew this at the time of Gurney's visit.

Gurney's visit had all the outward appearance of success. In America he saw and spoke to famous and powerful people. Many Friends received him enthusiastically. He aroused their enthusiasm for religious life and work. However, everywhere he went there were some who disapproved of his message. Opposition in Philadelphia and Ohio was vocal. The presence of Gurney and Stephen Grellet at Ohio Yearly Meeting in 1837 received only a mention in the minutes which is unusual in view of the importance of the two visitors. In New England John Wilbur and his supporters opposed Gurney at every chance. Gurney recognized some of the dissension. In his *Journal* he reported:

> ...In the Yearly Meeting [of New England] my return certificate was granted, notwithstanding a little appearance of contrary spirit...[6]

Gurney's return to England in 1840 did not stop Wilbur from preaching against "Gurneyism" and for a return to the primitive doctrines of Christianity. Wilbur's ideas made him oppose the ideas of the second Great Awakening and other "modern" ideas that included schools, canals and factories. Had he been willing to be relatively quiet, he might have been left alone. However, his vocal opposition to Gurney's supporters irritated some Friends and transformed them into opponents. They resolved to silence him and be rid of him.

The "evil moment" in which Wilbur's opponents committed "an astonishing instance of ecclesiastical oppression ... worthy of the dark precincts of papal tyranny"[7] came before Gurney had left for England. Matters moved slowly. First, a committee of Gurney's supporters in Rhode Island Quarterly Meeting investigated the problems of lack of unity there. This committee saw its task clearly. They called Wilbur in to account for his irritating behavior. Then they tried to get his monthly and preparative meetings to "deal with him." Wilbur's meeting, South Kingston Monthly Meeting, rejected the quarterly meeting's instruction. The quarterly meeting elders then found South Kingston to be insubordinate and declared it dissolved. Greenwich Monthly Meeting was given leave to absorb South Kingston's rights and powers. Greenwich quickly disowned John Wilbur from membership in the Society of Friends. John Wilbur appealed his case to the quarterly meeting. They divided on the issue, but did not split into separate groups at this time. In 1844 New England Yearly Meeting was faced with John Wilbur's disownment and a divided quarterly meeting. They agreed to sustain his disownment. In 1845, the yearly meeting received reports from two Rhode Island Quarterly Meetings.[8]

As in Philadelphia in 1827, and New York in 1828, the immediate focus of dissension in New England was over the identity of the clerk. At the 1845 yearly meeting a committee composed of representatives from both groups was named to bring forward the name of a new clerk and assistant clerk. The committee divided and each group united, separately, to bring names forward. The two sets of new appointees and the incumbents all tried to proceed with the business of the yearly meeting at the same time. The result was very noisy and quite unproductive. No yearly meeting before or since has ever had three simultaneous clerks.

By the next morning the Gurneyites agreed to stay with the old clerk and were in no mood to allow dissenters anything. When the Wilburite clerk, Thomas B. Gould, tried to get the use of the minute book he was rebuffed. About five hundred members withdrew. Fortunately, although feelings ran high, no physical violence was done.

After the 1845 yearly meeting, South Kingston Meeting was reconstituted, and John Wilbur was reinstated into full membership. He had never attended Greenwich Meeting. London and Dublin Yearly Meetings refused to recognize John Wilbur and his supporters, now called the "Smaller Body." They were given the same treatment given Hicksites. New York, Baltimore, North Carolina and

Indiana yearly meetings also recognized the "Larger Body," in spite of opposition. Ohio and Philadelphia tried to remain in correspondence with both bodies. Also, as in earlier divisions, the matter of rights to property was taken to court. The courts ruled in favor of the Gurneyite "Larger Body." [9]

In some ways the Wilbur separation is hard to understand. Theological issues were almost entirely limited to differences in emphasis. This had been recognized even at the height of the controversy. The differences at the time have been summed up nicely by Allen and Richard Thomas:

> ... [Wilbur] objected to Gurney's position that justification precedes sanctification, and maintained that a man is justified only as he is sanctified. The difference was really in the definition of terms, but the practical result of Wilbur's teaching is that the individual does not know that he is saved. John Wilbur also objected to any method of religious instruction but such as was directly prompted by the Spirit at the time, and believed that the giving of lectures on religious subjects, or the distinct teaching of Bible truth, as is done in Bible schools, was work done "in the Will of the creature." Gurney was active in supporting systematic Bible study, though he was as strong as anyone in upholding the necessity of immediate qualification and direct guidance in the ministry of the Word. In these points Wilbur was certainly nearer the Friends of the preceding century than Gurney ... [10]

Behind the theological difference were differences in life style. John Wilbur and his supporters were conservative farming Friends. They had survived the Revolution, seen the danger of Hicks and avoided his theological shortcomings. Conflicts at Lynn and New Bedford taught them that lesson. They were the old guard, and changes in the world disturbed them. Young people were leaving the farms to go to work in factories, or were moving west in large numbers. Gurney's evangelicalism was to them another radical change. He was just playing into the hands of those forcing the rapid pace of unwanted change. Wilbur was only fighting one of the many changes that was challenging the basis of his life. It took the driving force of the unstated changes to make the Wilburites into a coherent group.

The Gurneyites also had driving forces. Many New Englanders had been forced off the land because of its declining fertility and increased scarcity. They had either moved west or moved into the cities. They worked in the growing industrial and commercial enterprises, and were rewarded with greater wealth and security. A factory hand could work fewer hours a day and still earn more than a farmer could. This made Friends in the cities open to other changes. Education, prison reform, prohibition, slavery and women's rights all fitted nicely into the things Friends wanted to change. Joseph John Gurney, the wealthy, charming, well-known Englishman opened the way for them to be a little less of a "peculiar people." Gurney's arrival was welcomed as it allowed them to take part in at least two of the very strong current movements: evangelicalism and Bible study.

10

New England's Aftermath

New England's trauma was debated throughout the Orthodox branches of the Society of Friends. Discussions in most yearly meetings resulted in recognition for the larger body. This was formalized by the exchange of yearly meeting epistles. There were two exceptions to the almost complete neglect of the smaller, Wilburite, body in New England. These two exceptions were Ohio and Philadelphia.

A. Ohio Conservatives Go Their Own Way

At the start the disagreement in Ohio was basically the same as it had been in New England. In the debate, the question of which New England Yearly Meeting to recognize was overshadowed by the question of which New England epistles to read. In 1846 neither was read. This became the practice for several years. The clerk, Benjamin Hoyle, realized that he had simply delayed the matter.

By the late 1840s and early 1850s, the three things that had helped delay the conflict were overcome. The first, of course, was the issue of slavery. Once it was politically settled for Friends the other two became important. The first of these was that Ohio had a small but influential group in the middle between the Wilburite and Gurneyite proponents. Some Ohio Friends had seen the damage done by division and wanted to prevent the same sort of damage. They were helped by the fact that Ohio was still a pioneering rural society. The

89

social and economic differences between the the two extremes in Ohio were still relatively unimportant.

The Wilburite and Gurneyite groups were very similar in makeup and, unlike in New England, both lived in relative isolation. Yet, the religious differences between them were enough to serve as the basis for contention. Wilburites wanted to retain the ancient tradition of waiting in silence for the leadings of the Spirit. The others felt it was more important to return to the biblical basics as epitomized by Joseph John Gurney's teachings. The two groups also had other differences. They disagreed over whether Benjamin Hoyle should remain as clerk and they argued over which New England Yearly Meeting to recognize. In 1846 there was a visitor from the Wilburite New England body. His credentials were received after some debate. In 1853 it took four sittings of the yearly meeting to accept the credentials of a visitor from the Wilburites.

In 1854, the ninth year after the separation in New England and the year after the debate on credentials, everybody knew the issues: recognition of Benjamin Hoyle as clerk;[1] which New England epistle to read; and, the recognition of the credentials of visiting Friends. The visitors that year included Eliza P. Gurney, Joseph John Gurney's widow; William and Charles Evans from Philadelphia; and, Thomas B. Gould, the first yearly meeting clerk of the Wilburites, and his companion.

The turnout of Wilburites was far smaller than normal.[2] The change in the politics of slavery in effect took it off the yearly meeting agenda. Other things also affected the nature of the gathering. A cholera epidemic sweeping North American cities worried Friends enough to keep some of them away from Mount Pleasant that year. A drought also caused many of the farmers to stay home to feed and water their cattle. The combination was simply too much to avoid a good fight.

As one of the first items of business, a committee was appointed to come forward with the name of a new clerk. They failed to reach unity, something of a tradition by then. Benjamin Hoyle was proposed by the Wilburites and Jonathan Binns by the Gurneyites.

Also at the 1854 yearly meeting, the Wilburites favored accepting Gould's credentials. The Gurneyites opposed the idea because his companion was not a member of a select meeting. The final break came during the discussion of who should be clerk. Both sides insisted on their own and did it in the same place at the same time and from the same table.

Both sides claimed moral justification and both claimed to represent the "true" body. Hoyle's group sided with the Wilburite body in New England and Binns' with the Gurneyites. After the split, Binns' group received recognition from the Gurneyites in New England and by extension from most of the other Orthodox yearly meetings. Hoyle's group on the other hand simply withdrew from all official contact with other yearly meetings. They could not bring themselves to disown the Gurneyites in their meetings. Nor could they officially recognize other Wilburite bodies because they felt this would cut them off from the rest of the Society of Friends. The only exception was their willingness to give recognition of visiting ministers from Philadelphia. Both groups then acted as if they were repairing the damage done by separatists.

Describing events does not explain why Ohio Yearly Meeting chose 1854 to divide for a second time. The division could easily have happened at anytime after 1846. The issues had been the same for ten consecutive yearly meetings. That they did not go away or become less powerful as time went on is a measure of their importance. Yet we are left with trying to explain why the split did not happen in 1846 or in 1853 as it could so easily have done.

The key can be found in the presence of both Eliza P. Gurney and Thomas Gould at the same time. For once Ohio Yearly Meeting's activities and personalities were openly visible to two of the most important people from outside. They were visible to both the Gurneyite and the smaller Wilburite body in New England, and to both Philadelphia and London. The visitors were the embodiment of that difference. Everybody present understood this.

The easier task, once the presence of outsiders is seen as the causal factor, is to account for their presence at that particular yearly meeting. It was the first time so many visitors from so many yearly meetings were present. The answer is found in the development of railway connections between Ohio and the eastern seaboard. Up to the yearly meeting in 1853, the only ways to get to Ohio were by canal, post road, and river. All of these are slow, not much faster than traveling on foot. It took weeks to cover the distances. Rail links were slowly being built making travel easier, cheaper and much faster. In 1853 the last rail link between Cleveland and Pittsburgh was finished.[3] There were already several lines in Ohio, but1854 was the first year it was quick and easy for Friends from the Eastern states to get to Ohio Yearly Meeting. It was this that gave the Ohio Friends their sense of being visible to the outside. In sum, one can say that the final "straw" in this division was the steam engine.

Exposure alone would not have done it. It was visibility for people who had been quite isolated from each other as well as from Friends elsewhere. Small meetings build close ties. When people from small meetings gather in larger groups such as at yearly meeting, they take the strength of their ties with them. Every year for a decade there had been dissension over which New England body to recognize. This was overlaid by the more demanding issue, slavery, which had finally receded. However, in the older conflict each side was linked to people in New England. Relatives and friends in distant places often acquire a symbolic importance, especially when one is nostalgic for the home one left behind. To be frustrated in this when one is at an important gathering does little for friendly relationships.

Given the rules, being frustrated by not having their choice of clerk for eight consecutive yearly meetings served only to infuriate the Gurneyites. So, in 1854, when the important visitors from outside turned up and when the number of Wilburites was reduced, the issues came to a head. The Gurneyites had Eliza P. Gurney watching and listening. The Wilburites had Thomas Gould. This focused their anger, frustration and sense of self-righteousness. The division, then, was not surprising.

After the division, the two Ohio Yearly Meetings went their own ways. The Gurneyites became more evangelical and the Wilburites became more isolated. In his analysis of the results of the split in 1854, William Taber says that:

> ... the Wilburites lost not only the more activist of Ohio Yearly Meetings leaders, but also the usual channels by which cooperation, new life, and new ideas have always flowed from one Quaker group to another ... [4]

During the subsequent thirty year period the only visitors Wilburites would recognize officially were the ones from Philadelphia. Ohio Wilburites had only forty-five visitors in thirty years.[5]

The Civil War and then the loss of the school at Mount Pleasant to the Gurneyites in a law suit broke the last links between the Ohio Gurneyites and Wilburites. The school had been central to the Wilburite yearly meeting. The Wilburites then built their new school in Barnesville, and it became the new center for their yearly meeting. It revived interest in education and brought them out of their isolation. They began to discover other Conservative Friends as post Civil War divisions took place in other yearly meetings. The old school burned down shortly after it was reclaimed by the Gurneyites, and they never built another.

An interesting footnote to the two divisions in Ohio is that the title to the yearly meeting property in Mount Pleasant was, for a time, held by three Ohio yearly meetings. In 1883 the Wilburites transferred their interest in it to the Hicksites and in 1921 the Hicksites transferred theirs to the Gurneyites. Finally, Gurneyite Friends deeded the property in 1950 to the State of Ohio as a historical building.[6]

B. Philadelphia Hangs Together

The effect in Philadelphia of Joseph John Gurney's visit was quite different. Right from the beginning, he had not been unanimously welcomed. Many had grave reservations about his teachings and the apparent worldliness he represented. They were even less happy when they learned that his letter of clearness to travel had not been given him in unity. Furthermore, events in New England did nothing to endear him to them. His supporters were seen as having mistreated John Wilbur in a very unfortunate way.

Ohio's division reminded them of the pain of the earlier divisions in Philadelphia and New England. The events in those two yearly meetings had been discussed at great length. Philadelphia too, faced having to decide which epistles to receive. There were supporters of both sides. Some meetings were very sympathetic to Wilbur and others were followers of Gurney.

Samuel Bettle, who had been the clerk at the fatal yearly meeting in 1827, was the leader of the group that worked very hard to keep the yearly meeting together this time. Philadelphia had defended the Wilburites in New England in 1849 and recognized the Wilburite body in Ohio in 1855. Philadelphia was always careful not to rescind the Wilburite recognition. Bettle regreted his part in the earlier separation and pled to remain undivided.[7]

The strongly Wilburite editors of *The Friend* argued the unsoundness of Gurney's teachings.[8] They described the lack of unity in England over Gurney's journey and expressed the feeling that settling on Binns as clerk of the yearly meeting in Ohio was "a violation of the discipline and usages of the society."[9] They were supported by the members of the Arch Street Meeting in Philadelphia. The Gurneyites, who were in opposition, apparently were centered at the 12th Street Meeting in the same city. Their counter-argument was that unless they recognized the Gurneyites in Ohio and in New England, they would be cut off from all other Friends bodies. Howard Brinton describes the differences between Wilburites and Gurneyites as:

...not superficial. The Wilburites emphasized right experience as essential to salvation, the Gurneyites right belief. The Gurneyites accused the Wilburites of being "mystics." The Wilburites accused the Gurneyites of subscribing to an intellectual religion "afloat on the surface."...[10]

The stormy argument went on for several years. In 1854 a small group of Wilburite Friends withdrew from Baltimore Yearly Meeting to form a new Baltimore Yearly Meeting of Primitive Friends. After more argument in 1858 Philadelphia Friends decided to eliminate all correspondence with other yearly meetings. This allowed them to avoid objections to reading the New England epistles and let them "hang together." They did not want another division, as the first was still very painful. They were also careful never to withdraw recognition of the Wilburite bodies. Instead a constant exchange of ministers was maintained with both sides.

It is clear that the injury done by the 1827 division was enough to make Philadelphia Friends very reluctant to allow a second. Further, the sympathies for the two sides were strong, especially for the New England Wilburites. Philadelphia Friends carefully controlled where visitors were taken. Wilburites were usually taken to the Arch Street Meeting and then went from there to other Wilburite meetings. Visitors from London Yearly Meeting and from the Gurneyite bodies went to the 12th. Street Meeting. They recognized the likelihood of conflict and simply sent visitors to the meetings that would be most congenial to them.[11] These practices were kept up until 1924, after which epistles were sent to Friends everywhere.

C. Primitive Friends

The separating Friends in Baltimore established their yearly meeting in 1854 with William Waring as clerk.[12] They recognized the Wilburite group in Ohio[13] and adjourned to meet in the house of Joseph J. Hopkins, because the group was so small.[14] Thereafter they corresponded only with other Wilburite bodies. This caused them trouble in giving and receiving certificates of removal from other yearly meetings.

From then on only the most routine of tasks were reported in their minutes: the Queries were answered, often with exactly the same wording they had used the year before. Their minutes, which is the only thing I discovered, were devoid of statements about activities or concerns. After their decision to form their own meeting they did no more than decide to meet once again at the next appointed time. During the Civil War, living in what was a Southern city occupied by

Northern troops, no mention was made of the war. On the issue of slavery, their response to the Query was always:

> Friends appear careful to bear a testimony against slavery. Those of African race under their direction are suitably provided for and instructed in useful learning.[15]

There was no mention of the end of the war, just as there had been none during it. Nor was there mention of the then very contentious Emancipation Proclamation. After 1865 the group was so small it ceased to function.

11

Fritchley
and
Manchester

All the American troubles were reported to English Friends. They felt isolated from them and did what they thought best to help and, at the same time, to avoid involvement. The Beaconite controversy made it evident that this was not always possible. Quaker evangelicalism had not vanished just because Beaconite Friends went their own way. Crewdson's beliefs had not been all that different from Joseph John Gurney's. Gurney allowed for the gentle leadings of the Spirit, something Crewdson rejected. Otherwise, they were quite similar. Now in the latter part of the nineteenth century, London Yearly Meeting was also to face problems from two extremes of Quakerism.

A. Fritchley, The Conservative Extreme

When John Wilbur was in England in 1831-33 he had been given a warm reception by some English Friends. These Friends were the ones who later had opposed the idea of Joseph John Gurney's trip to America. One of the English conservatives made a return trip to New England in the 1860s to learn from Wilbur's followers. This man, John G. Sargeant, had gone through an act of conversion that had transformed him from nominal membership. He was concerned about the changes that made much of the Discipline optional. He wanted Friends to keep to the letter of the Discipline. He wanted Friends to retain all of the symbols that set them apart and made them into a peculiar people. He was afraid that change would lead to laxity of behavior.

There is some very persuasive evidence that Friends did not all behave as was expected. A former Friend described how she had observed Friends who obeyed the Testimony against the paying of tithes and, at the same time, got credit for having paid their tithes. The mechanism was simple: goods were seized from Friends who were found guilty of refusal to pay their tithes. When they also refused to pay fines, their goods, normally the household's sterling silver, were seized. The goods were then sold publicly to cover the fine. The goods were usually bought by a silversmith. The silver was cleaned and repaired and then the Friends from whom it was originally seized were offered the opportunity of buying it back. The price paid covered the cost of the fine and the silversmith's work. As the same smiths bought the silver each time it was sold publicly, and they knew the Friends from whom it was seized, they could feel sure of a profit. In return the Friends got their silver cleaned and repaired. These Friends were also credited with payment of their fine and tithe by proxy without running afoul of the Discipline.

The woman who wrote the book was eventually disowned for her critical views of the elders who behaved in this fashion. She was quite disillusioned by Friends as she wrote:

> To consider the Society of Friends as a religious body, is a monstrous stretch of the imagination. Respectable, active, intelligent, benevolent, useful, wealthy and influential, they undoubtedly are; but a man may be all this, and yet devoid of that religion, without which he can never hope for life eternal...[1]

John Sargeant was offended by behavior such as this, and he was also offended by the evangelicalism that had crept into English Quakerism.[2] Other British Friends shared Sargeant's concern over the liberalizing tendencies in London Yearly Meeting. They began to hold a series of conferences in 1862 that were attended by only a few Friends. In 1864 a group of them moved to the village of Fritchley and, without official sanction, set up their own monthly meeting. In 1868 Sargeant visited the Wilburite bodies in America for a second time and returned to England full of determination to preserve Friends true and ancient ways. The conservatives who had remained in England were divided by his actions. Some opposed him and others did not. After two more conferences, one in September 1868 and another in October, 1869, some agreed to withdraw with him to form their own Fritchley General Meeting, named after the small village they had chosen to move to.

This new General Meeting was quite indistinguishable from other Friends groups but for its anachronistic dress and speech.[3] Like the Wilburites, they retained the central Quakerism Friends had always had. And, unlike the Primitive Friends in Baltimore, they did not lose the important theological basis of Quakerism. However, this withrawal was a quiet one of relatively unimportant people and, hence, went almost unnoticed.

Early this century half of the body of Fritchley Friends, about forty of them, migrated to Canada. They settled on the bank of the North Saskatchewan River, some fifty miles from Saskatoon. Once settled they joined Canada Yearly Meeting (Conservative) and were brought back into a larger body of Friends, one compatible with their ideals. In 1955, the three yearly meetings in Canada, the Conservative, Orthodox and Genessee Yearly Meetings, came together to form Canadian Yearly Meeting.[4] Fritchley Friends (now Borden Friends) found themselves back in a yearly meeting that had the same problems that had caused them to withdraw from London Yearly Meeting a century earlier. The few remaining in Borden did not feel comfortable with the new yearly meeting, so they withdrew again. The minute of Canadian Yearly Meeting at the time of the withdrawal reads:

> We heard with sorrow the decision of Halcyonia Monthly Meeting to be unassociated with Canadian Yearly Meeting. Although our formal association may be terminated we treasure the ties of friendship and intervisitation we have with Friends in Borden and hope these will remain strong.[5]

Muriel Bishop, Canadian Yearly Meeting Recording Clerk at the time, wrote in a note appended to the copy of the minute:

> I believe the decision had to do with theological differences and the strong links between Borden Friends and the Moral Rearmament Movement.[6]

While the Canadian remnant of Fritchley was withdrawing, the English remnant was going in the other direction. London Yearly Meeting had approached them on a number of occasions to attempt a reunification. These visits bore fruit. In October, 1967 Fritchley Friends decided to give up their separate organization and rejoin London Yearly Meeting.[7] The happy reunion between Fritchley

Friends and London Yearly Meeting contrasts with the withdrawal in Canada. The vast Canadian distances and the small number of Friends in Canada made contact with Borden both fleeting and infrequent. There, the bonds that might have been forged through more frequent contact were not made. In England, the efforts of a few Friends over a long period of time had created the ties that brought Friends back together.

B. Manchester: The Modern Extreme

At about the same time at the other end of the political spectrum were David Duncan and his group of students. His free-thinking religious ideas were leading to a noisy disownment of a group almost as large as that in Fritchley. David Duncan was a convinced Friend and former Presbyterian minister. He was the leader of a group of fifty to eighty young members of the Mount Street Meeting in Manchester, England. They were a part of the adult education movement in which Friends had become involved. They met regularly in the evenings to study new ideas.

David Duncan had become intrigued with the ideas in a book entitled *Essays and Reviews*[8] which he presented to this study group in 1861. He felt it gave the group a look at some new ideas that would let them examine the bases of their faith. The book was a collection of the latest ideas in literary criticism applied to the Bible, biblical archeology and biology. The ideas clearly upset some older Friends, among them J. Bevan Braithwaite.

The Beacon controversy had hit Braithwaite as a young man in his twenties; David Duncan's "heresy" came when he was fifty. Braithwaite had just returned from a visit to Friends in America. He had seen the devastation of war and had visited Indiana, Iowa, Western and Baltimore Yearly Meetings. He was involved with the British and Foreign Bible Society and was a founder of the Friends Foreign Mission Association[9]. With all this on his mind, he was really not ready to deal gently with David Duncan when the yearly meeting asked him to.

Crewdson's earlier withdrawal had divided and hurt many wealthy and active families. It had pushed Friends to be more aware of their biblical heritage and had encouraged many to make the Bible the ultimate authority. With such emphasis, the meaning of Christ's death upon the Cross had become central. Gurney's inspiration was shared by others, many of whom were influential in London Yearly Meeting.

The pain experienced by these wealthy and influential evangelicals during the Beacon experience and the re-examination of their beliefs that it forced had fixed their ideas. Braithwaite wrote that he had emerged from the earlier controversy:

> ... with all his religious opinions thoroughly grounded and settled. He loved his Savior from a child, and having once made up his mind that the Society of Friends embodied in its belief the fundamental truths of Christianity ... he never ... wavered in his allegiance to it...[10]

J. Bevan Braithwaite was the unofficial leader of the committee appointed by London Yearly Meeting to look into the disturbances in Manchester. The committee was dominated by evangelicals. They set out to investigate the complaints against David Duncan's wide-ranging challenge to evangelical ideas. Richenda Scott saw David Duncan as:

> ... a thoughtful, widely-read man, a strong advocate of social reform, of universal education, of large and all-embracing views of humanity rather than of loyalty to sect, class or creed, republican, that is left wing, in his political views ... [He] had come into prominence in the Society by a lecture given at Manchester Institute in 1861 on the famous volume of Essays and Reviews published the previous year ...[11]

Duncan had said: "There is one feature common to all the Essays — the recognition of the inward light — and it is curious to remember that the attacks with which early Friends were assailed, were characterized by the same assertions of impiety and heresy."[12] For this and his earlier ideas David Duncan was attacked, questioned and asked to recant. When he refused to do so in 1871, he was disowned.

Duncan died of smallpox the next year before he could appeal his disownment. Eleven of his followers resigned almost immediately, and several followed later. Together they started their own meeting for worship with an attendance of about forty. The meeting lasted for a few years and published a monthly paper called the Manchester Friend. They were characterized by their intellectual freedom, lack of hierarchy and organization, and by the informality of their discussion.[13]

C. Conclusion

On the surface the two English divisions are like the earlier

American explosions, but they were more like the divisions that were yet to come in America. In England, Friends evangelical thought combined social change and flexibility with theological orthodoxy and rigidity. The social change had driven Fritchley Friends to set up their own meeting protected by rural isolation. At the same time the theological orthodoxy of English Friends could not allow them to accept David Duncan's explorations. Social change was encouraged by evangelicalism; yet, revelation from scriptural infallibility did not combine well with the kinds of modern German biblical scholarship. The theory of evolution was one focal point of the controversy. David Duncan challenged evangelical Friends to consider this theory and reintroduce an idea, out of favor among leading Friends for over thirty years: the idea of the Inner Light as a source of religious inspiration. This challenge was met and the idea expunged — if only momentarily — from English Quakerism.

Crewdson had set the stage for both the Fritchley and Manchester divisions. The former was a withdrawal by people opposed to change, and the second a disownment of people who wanted change. Bevan Braithwaite's family had been divided by the Beaconite division, which may have made him less than willing to tolerate David Duncan's challenge. The trauma of the earlier division combined with Victorian growth and prosperity to close the doors to creative religious thought for many. At the same time, the rigid Quaker codes of dress and language were being loosened. David Duncan's followers reacted to the rigid religious thought and Fritchley Friends tried to preserve the tradition in dress and language. In a sense these two small groups fell off opposite ends of the religious-social continuum.

That Fritchley and New England conservatives were similar is incidental. They were each unique in their own place and time. In New England they were rural conservatives. In England they were conservatives who became rural. The reintroduction of an old idea, combined with a host of new ideas by David Duncan, forced Friends to either expunge the whole or face a re-thinking of the theology painfully thought through at an earlier time.

After the Civil War in the American Midwest

12

Social Change
in Indiana

After the Civil War various legislative acts, notably the Morril Act that gave land for the support of university education, and the Homestead Act that gave land to settlers who opened it to farming, combined with Indian wars, the emancipation of both blacks and Indians, and construction of the railroads to transform Mid-Western society. Women became deeply involved in the changes and formed the Women's Suffrage Association in 1869, the same year the Prohibition Party was formed. These were followed by the organization of the Women's Christian Temperance Union in 1874 and the Anti-Saloon League in 1893. Women Friends pioneered in all these causes.

Quakers were also deeply affected by the changes that were introduced by the evangelical movement and the closely linked holiness movement. The evangelical movement, begun among the Methodists, became typical of the West. It moved East in the years between 1840 and 1857. Before the Civil War, Presbyterians became affected by it even though there were strong anti-revival feelings in some rural sections of the church.[1] Revivals were a central part of the movement. Timothy Smith, for example, regards the revival as "The cutting edge of American Christianity after 1850..."[2] Friends became involved deeply in this movement. However, they became prominent in the Holiness movement after the Civil War. Melvin Dieter gives prominence in this movement to Robert Pearsall and Hannah Whitehall Smith for having "... ignited the holiness revival movement in

England..."[3] Dieter also saw Dougan Clark and Hulda Rese as "...founders of the International Apostolic Holiness Union which later became the Pilgrim Holiness Church ..."[4]

At first these two movements had a greater effect on the content than on the form of Friends worship. The Bible was re-emphasized after what had come to be regarded as a tragic loss of its importance. A study was done by the Bible Association of Friends in 1832. In this they found that four hundred families in the Orthodox body " ... were without a complete copy of Scriptures, while one hundred and thirty-eight had not even a New Testament ..."[5]

When the form of Friends worship changed they were guided by the forms introduced in the "The Awakening of 1858."[6] T. L. Smith summarized the change nicely:

> The mid-century revivals brought to a climax four fundamental changes in the inner life of American Protestantism. The traditional predominance of the clergy ... now gave place rapidly to ... lay participation and control. The spirit of interdenominational brotherhood ... came swiftly to maturity and caught the imagination of the greatest churchmen of the land. Ethical concerns replaced dogmatic zeal in evangelical preaching and writing. And, equally important, Arminian views crowded out Calvinism in much of the dogma which remained.[7]

The importance of women in the new movements, the sense of disciplined control of behavior and the lay participation appealed very strongly to Friends in the Midwest.[8]

Friends, as a body, had a delayed reaction to both the evangelical and the holiness movements. They had been deeply affected by the conflict between their anti-slavery ideals and their ideals on war. The result produced a reaction that led to both a renewal of the anti-war sentiments and a drive toward religious change.[9] When they did react to the religious changes around them, they did so with great fervor. While they became more like non-Friends in religious behavior, they also lost their fervor for disciplining each other for behavioral infractions. The frequency with which they disowned members dropped to a small fraction of what it had been before the war.[10] Most important from our point of view here, they began to hold prayer meetings of their own and increased their efforts in the missions. In 1860, at Indiana Yearly Meeting, Friends received a request from their young people to hold prayer meetings. This was renewed after the Civil War. In 1867 the yearly meeting approved a proposal to hold General Meetings for "Divine worship."

106

Charles Coffin described the first of these meetings in the following way:

> When the meeting began the announcement was made that the meeting was for young people and was in their hands. Several of the signers of the request made short addresses. But then came an absolutely unlooked-for and marvelous outpouring. There was absolutely no urging to speak, no calls for converts to rise. Everything was orderly. But more than 150 people either prayed, or rose to tell of their intention to serve their Master, and their desire to become Christ's children. The meeting lasted from seven o'clock until midnight and was difficult to close even then.[11]

By 1881 more than one hundred places were reported to have held prayer meetings, which they chose to call General Meetings, which lasted from two to forty-nine days.[12] With General Meetings came rapid growth in the size of the meetings and a concern over the disparity between the numbers professing conversion and the number of new members.[13] The number of people who professed conversion in Indiana Yearly Meeting between 1881 and 1888 totaled 22,420, and the number of new members was 9,158. At no time in the history of the yearly meeting had there been a more rapid increase of membership.[14] It became the largest gathering of Friends and remained so in spite of the new yearly meetings they set off. Western Yearly Meeting became a separate yearly meeting in 1858; Iowa Yearly Meeting in 1863; Kansas Yearly Meeting in 1872; and, Wilmington Yearly Meeting in 1892.

During this period a new system developed that deeply affected the Society of Friends. It was the gradual appearance of a system of paid pastoral ministry. It grew by a series of small steps into a major force for change. It began simply with a means to prevent the loss of new converts. Statements of Friends beliefs were written and specially chosen Friends were "released" to look after the converts. The practice of "releasing" Friends grew out of general meetings in a quiet way. Friends who had ministered well in one meeting were often asked to do it for others. They soon realized this made it hard to keep a job or run a farm since the meetings lasted several days at a time. Hence, Friends began the practice of covering both travel costs and living costs as well. Finally, some of the more successful ministers were asked to stay on permanently in the places they had led successful gatherings, to care for the newly convinced Friends.[15]

Another reason for the creation of the pastoral system is given by Brinton. He wrote:

It has often been suggested that the pastoral system with its programmed worship came into the Society of Friends because of failure of the meeting based on silence and particularly failure of the older type of ministry. This may, in some instances, have been true, but in the great majority of cases it appears to have come, not because of absence of Life, but because of too much liveliness. The Revival unsettled the meeting, produced a chaos of ecstatic testimonies and much running about, and the pastor was brought in to restore order. The more active aggressive element also welcomed his assumption of responsibility to lessen the influence of the more pacific conservative element.[16]

Although I am persuaded by arguments based on liveliness, which all three men share, I am not persuaded by the argument based on numbers as the events followed in a different order. First, in 1860, was the demand from the young people for a new form of worship. It was in keeping with the practices of other religious bodies they had observed and shared. By 1861, minister's wages were reported to the yearly meeting, a thing repeated in 1864 again in 1866, 1871, 1873 and in 1878.[17] The change in the Discipline came at this time from the demands of the young people. It was after this that the growth in numbers began. I came to the same conclusion about the changes in North Carolina Yearly Meeting at a later date.[18]

The names of the earliest Friends pastors include Robert W. Douglas, Nathan and Esther Frame, all of whom were appointed as early as 1861.[19] The first Friend called "pastor" was Elkanah Beard who was elected pastor by the members of a non-denominational Union Camp Church.[20] The first person to be named a Quaker pastor possibly as early as 1872 was Luke Woodward.[21] At any rate, the number of Quaker Pastors grew quickly and became enough of an embarrassment that in 1878 the query on "hireling priests" was omitted at Indiana Yearly Meeting. A statement on the support of the ministry was substituted.

In 1896 Walnut Ridge, Wabash, and Winchester Quarterly Meetings asked that the system of a paid ministry be officially endorsed by the yearly meeting.[22] Agreement came, but the change was met with considerable opposition.[23] Curiously, just as the pastoral system gained acceptance, the increase in membership slowed down.[24]

Another request for change came from new members and younger Friends who wanted music to go with their worship. Soon, pianos and organs appeared in the same meetings that had pastors. If pastors and music in meetings caused discomfort, the evangelical prayer meetings Friends held caused even more distress. Older Friends tried to control matters by refusing permission to hold prayer meetings. However, the elders could not prevent prayer meetings when they were organized by visiting Friends carrying minutes from their own meetings.

As Friends came closer to their neighbors in their religious practice, the firmness of their views on other ceremonies was challenged. In their traditional practice the sacraments of the Eucharist and Baptism had been totally rejected. Friends considered that by living in the Light they were leading essentially sacramental lives. Hence, the Eucharist and Baptism as special ceremonies were unnecessary. By the end of the Civil War these issues had been met and dealt with, "for the last time!" when Elisha Bates was disowned in Ohio. His disownment came in 1836 for having been baptized.[25] Bates' disownment did not make this idea go away. It came back years later with greater force during the time of David B. Updegraff.

The changes created turmoil and led to divisions into orthodox and conservative meetings. The orthodox meetings were to retain and build on their Gurneyite traditions, while the conservative meetings came to resemble the Wilburites. Iowa and Western Yearly Meetings divided in 1877 and Kansas in 1879. Canada had a division that began in 1879 and was completed in 1881. Perhaps the best summary of the objections to the changes was written by Joel Bean, an Iowa conservative Friend. He had been present during the troubles in Iowa and complained that the Orthodox held beliefs which included:

A theory of Salvation is widely taught and accepted in which repentance and works of any kind seem to have no necessary part.

Salvation 'full and free;' i. e., salvation not only from the guilt of sin, to all the fullness of Christian perfection, seems perpetually to be taught as a thing fully wrought out and purchased for us by the blood of Christ, and offered for our simple acceptance by faith alone. Complete sanctification is claimed as a definite experience, instantaneously received, and defined to be 'the eradication, not merely the subjugation of the disposition to sin,' in which our bodily propensities are restored to their normal action ... [26]

The divisions alarmed Indiana Friends, but even more alarming to them was Dougan Clark's baptism in 1894.[27] Dougan Clark was a professor at Earlham College and an important member of the yearly meeting. This event combined with the others to give Indiana Friends the feeling that Friends were drifting into changes that would lead them into a disaster, changes that violated their views of what made them distinctive. The need for a unifying experience had appeared as early as 1860. It grew and led to Indiana Yearly Meeting's call for a general conference of Friends to be held in 1887.[28] Invitations were sent to all the yearly meetings with which they exchanged epistles. Wilburite and Hicksite Friends were not invited largely because they were not recognized as Friends. The invitation to attend the conference was accepted by representatives from Indiana, London, Dublin, New England, Baltimore, North Carolina, Ohio, New York, Western, Iowa, Canada, and Kansas Yearly Meetings.[29]

The most controversial result of this conference was the production of a Declaration of Faith.[30] This statement was the work of a special committee headed by the English Friend, J. Bevan Braithwaite. The major part of it took only a few days as it was a compilation of statements from earlier yearly meeting minutes.[31] In its concluding minute the 1887 conference asked the following question: "Is it desirable that all the Yearly Meetings of Friends [except the Wilburites and Hicksites] in the world should adopt one declaration of Christian doctrine?"[32] They answered the question in the affirmative. They assumed Friends used the Bible as the basis for their faith. They also refused to transform the Declaration into a creed. The chairman of the conference said:

> Undoubtedly this declaration is in entire harmony with that of all the Yearly Meetings in the world, and an acceptance of this would not of necessity suspend the declarations which they already have. But it would be an expression of the united views which all the Yearly Meetings have.[33]

The controversy over the declaration began before the conference was over. A prominent Ohio Friend, David B. Updegraff, raised the question of the freedom of yearly meetings to accept the declaration as given. In response to the question, James Wood, the chairman of the conference assured Ohio Friends that "... every Yearly Meeting is perfectly independent in its action ..."[34] David Updegraff's objections were about the absence of any reference to "... the matters of the baptism and the supper ... " He warned the conference that the declaration would be "... open to the most minute scrutiny and investigation ..." and would be rejected.[35]

At the subsequent conference in 1892 they produced a Uniform Discipline to be adopted by all of the yearly meetings. By 1902 eleven yearly meetings had accepted the Uniform Discipline as theirs. On the basis of this they agreed to form a new body called the Five Years Meeting.

110

Ohio Yearly Meeting did not join Five Years Meeting partly because of the efforts of David B. Updegraff. David Updegraff was born in Ohio in 1830. He went through a conversion experience in 1860. He was disowned by his Conservative meeting in 1865 for uniting with the Gurneyites. He went through a second conversion experience in 1869 shortly before he began his ministry.[36] In this second experience Updegraff claimed to have experienced "entire sanctification."[37] He was baptized with water in 1882. This was consistent with his stand on the practice of ordinances: communion and baptism. He felt that early Friends' stance against these two practices resulted from the insistence by the Church of England which had forced them into the practices. His reading of the Bible led him to believe that the practice of the sacraments was universally commanded, as they were ordained by Jesus.[38]

"Entire sanctification," above, refers to the feeling the person has who undergoes the experience of being made holy and entirely free from the power of sin. It is the second level of spiritual change. The first, conversion, is also referred to as either being "saved" or "justified." At this stage the meaning of Christ's sacrifice on the Cross is brought home to the person. The third stage is that of "glorification" and corresponds to the ascension into Heaven at the death of the believer.[39]

Updegraff was not alone in his views of salvation, sanctification, baptism and the eucharist, among the Ohio Friends, but he also met with fierce opposition. There was debate in the yearly meeting on baptism and the eucharist, the "ordinances" as they came to be called. Updegraff's views lost out and almost resulted in a third division in Ohio. However, he did retain a great deal of influence. He represented Ohio at the Richmond Conference in 1887 and again in 1892. The strength of his views on the ordinances and the stand taken by the conference explains, in part, why Ohio never became part of the Five Years Meeting.

13

Iowa's
Quaker Multiplicity

The history of Friends in the State of Iowa is complicated. Almost lost in it is the history of the few Hicksite Friends who followed the great migrations from the East. They came from Virginia just before the Civil War in 1856. Friends from Fairfax Quarterly Meeting in Virginia established Prairie Grove Monthly Meeting. In 1866 Wapinonoc Monthly Meeting was established, making it the second monthly meeting in Iowa. The two monthly meetings then united in a quarterly meeting under Baltimore Yearly Meeting.[1] The distance and growing number of Friends led to a joint committee of Indiana and Baltimore Yearly Meetings to recommend in 1875 that they be set apart, with other Midwestern Hicksite meetings, they to form Illinois Yearly Meeting.[2]

Not as obscure in history is the group of Ohio Wilburites. Friends such as "...two Hampton brothers, Joseph Edgerton, Francis William, Jesse North, William P. Deweese and William P. Bedell..." are mentioned by Errol Elliott as among the first to move to Iowa.[3] Along with other Friends they may have moved to Iowa as early as 1850. It was not long before the new meetings joined to form Hickory Grove Quarterly Meeting under Ohio Yearly Meeting (Wilburite). Scattergood School, near West Branch, was opened in 1890.

A third group of Quakers to move to Iowa was composed of Norwegian Friends, looking for a place to escape the restrictions placed on them by life in Norway. Some had gone to America as early as 1825.[4] In 1856 Anna Ravnaas traveled to America with Ole Tow. They were joined by Soren Olson in Salem, Iowa. Shortly after Soren Olson and Anna Ravnaas were married they moved to Marshal County, the place that was to become the largest center for Norwegian Quakers in America, and helped form Stavanger meeting.[5]

The fourth and largest of the groups of Friends were the Orthodox Friends, the first to arrive, in 1835. The first Quaker family, Isaac Pidgeon, his wife and seven children, was soon followed by Aaron Street and Peter Boyer. Together they settled to form a meeting for worship and monthly meeting at Salem, Iowa. In 1838 the first monthly meeting was established there by Vermillion Quarterly Meeting of Indiana Yearly Meeting.[6] The number of Orthodox Friends grew rapidly, and in 1863 Iowa Yearly Meeting was set off by Indiana. By this time they were already beginning to feel the effects of evangelicalism. In 1861 Joel Bean, a prominent Iowa Friend, wrote a letter to Rufus Jones:

> ... The revival began with a genuine and deepening work of Grace ... The subjects of Holiness and Perfection were in the the air, and engaging earnest attention among Christians everywhere ... Our own minds and hearts were in full sympathy with the rising tide of Christian thought and aspiration ... [7]

Soon after, this "rising tide" began to get out of the elders' control. In early 1865 a group that called itself "The Christian Vigilance Band" was organized by the students of Center Grove Academy, with the purpose of promoting revival. Shortly after a group like it came into being at Whittier College.[8] Joel Bean wrote in the British *Friend* some years later about the events in the following way:

> Many who were amongst the readiest to welcome signs of revival in our Society (using the word in its true sense), and who laboured earnestly and devotedly to promote it, have had to stand aloof from the movement, where it has adopted means which they felt to be hazardous and scattering to the Church and defeating to the very object desired.[9]

He followed it with the summary of theological objections quoted in the previous chapter.

Older Friends tried to control matters by refusing permission to hold prayer meetings. This only stopped those organized by their young people. However, prayer meetings organized by visiting Friends with minutes from their own meetings could not be stopped, because minutes were not given lightly and could not be ignored by members of other meetings.

The first major incident in Iowa Yearly Meeting was the one at Bear Creek in 1867. Stacy Bevan from Honey Creek and John S. Bond from Bangor Monthly Meeting, both from Iowa, with minutes from their home meetings, were on their way through Iowa to visit Kansas Friends. They stopped and held a public meeting, " ... where the power of the Lord was wonderfully manifest ... [10] Some older Friends, upset by these events tried to close the gathering but were unable to do so. The traveling Friends were instructed by the elders to go back to their home meetings which they refused to do. Instead, in spite of the large dose of "elder tea" they went ahead with their prayer meetings.

The term "elder tea" was used to downplay the seriousness of the "eldering," or disciplining, the visitors received at the hands of the elders who were displeased with them. Friends who misbehaved were "eldered" for their misdeeds. Such was taken with great seriousness by all concerned. Using this form is an indication of the gulf that was beginning to open between the young visiting ministers and the elders of the meetings they visited.

As prayer meetings grew in popularity they came to be called general meetings. In 1872 a yearly meeting committee was struck to oversee them. The next year one general meeting was held in each of the quarterly meetings of Iowa Yearly Meeting. They were able to report that: "Much good order prevailed, yet a few exceptions to be regretted." The frequency and length of these meetings increased with reports of "great satisfaction."[11]

With the increased number of general meetings went an increase in the number of newly organized monthly meetings. To answer to their needs for pastoral care, Iowa Friends amended their Discipline to create "a committee on pastoral care" for each meeting. By yearly meeting in 1876 nine of the ten quarterly meetings were able to report that they had complied.[12]

Frontier life put great loads on the committees who usually found one person to carry their responsibilities. These people had to be freed financially to do the work because nobody had the resources to do it without help. Pragmatic decisions to help ministering Friends grew into invitations to have them prolong their visits. This, in turn, grew into a new practice of "hireling ministry" which violated long standing and strongly felt principles. By 1871 two quarterly meetings reported they were not "clear" concerning their use of "hireling ministry." Three quarterly meetings were in violation of the principle in 1874. The frequency of such violations increased, and in 1876 the

Discipline was revised. Reference to the testimony for the "freedom of the Gospel Ministry" was deleted.[13] The new Query 7 now read:

> Are there any known cases of a breach of our Testimony against war, against all swearing, lotteries, and against the use, manufacture or traffic in intoxicating liquors, except for medicinal or mechanical purposes?

In February, 1877, a revival that lasted from Sunday to Wednesday was held immediatedly after Bear Creek Quarterly Meeting. This was the same place that had served "elder tea" ten years earlier. On the last day of the revival there was an altar call that led to a great deal of confusion. Many of the elders were deeply upset; some left in tears.

Friends who had been most distressed called a conference for early 1877 to maintain "our ancient doctrines and principles." They appointed a clerk for the day and produced a document with their objections. It began with the complaint that there was:

> ... a drawing away from the spirituality of the gospel ... to settle down ... in a literal knowledge and belief of the truths of the Holy Scriptures.

They went on with their list to say they were disturbed by:

> ... untempered zeal by taking up one particular truth;... a tendency to undervalue the writings of Ancient Friends ... The introduction into meetings for worship of much formality in the way of reading and singing and in the character of the ministry and prayer ... giving unmistakable evidence that it is the product of the intellect ... other than proceeding from the immediate inspiration of the true Shepherd of the sheep ... Leaders being selected to conduct the exercises who many times point out and dictate services. Also the introduction of the mourners's bench and the manner of consecration, the disorder, confusion and exciting scenes attending many of them, wherein the young and inexperienced are urged to give expressions to their overwrought feelings in a manner inconsistent with our principles[14]

At the end of the conference they sent a letter to Bear Creek Monthly Meeting of Friends, signed by Zimri Horner, in which they stated:

> At a conference of Friends ... it was decided that the time had fully come when it was incumbent upon us in order to support our

ancient doctrines and principles to disclaim the offices of the nondescript body now in church government, and replace them by those in unity with the doctrines and in favor of supporting our ancient principles and testimonies.[15]

The separation between Orthodox and Conservative Friends, started at North Branch Monthly Meeting on the 16th of June, spread to Bear Creek on the 30th and then Summit Grove. These three meetings then prepared reports for the quarterly meeting held in Bear Creek on the 12th of August. Two reports were sent on to the yearly meeting in Oskaloosa on the 5th of September, 1877. One report was signed by Zimri Horner and the other by Jesse W. Kenworthy and Cathrine R. Hadley.

Two reports from two Bear Creek Quarterly Meetings forced the yearly meeting into a quandary. They referred the matter to the Representatives who reported back to the effect that they were: "... entirely united that the reports signed by Jesse W. Kenworthy and Catherine R. Hadley as clerks, are the reports of Bear Creek Quarterly Meeting."[16] In other words, the yearly meeting chose to recognize the Orthodox group, a group that had actively conducted prayer meetings.

The yearly meeting, now without Conservative Friends, appointed a committee to visit Bear Creek and look into the matter. Their report delivered the following year suggested that the Separatists be treated as if they had joined another religious body.[17] Orthodox Friends were also careful to make certain they retained the meeting property by incorporating Bear Creek Monthly Meeting.[18]

Only enough conservatives separated to form two quarterly meetings. The founding of West Branch Quarterly Meeting in 1883 gave the Conservatives a third quarterly meeting. In the opening minute of their first yearly meeting, held in Oskaloosa, Iowa, on Ninth month 7th., 1877, written by Zimri Horner, Clerk, they agreed:

> In consideration of the various departures in doctrine and principle and practice brought into our beloved Society of late years by modern innovators, who have so revolutionized our ancient order of the church as to run into views and practices out of which our early Friends were led, and into a broader and more self-pleasing and cross-shunning way than that marked out by our Savior and held by our Ancient Friends, and who have so approximated to the unregenerated word that we feel it incumbent upon us to bear testimony against all such degenerate innovations in order to maintain our ancient doctrines, principles and practices and sustain the

church for the purpose for which it was peculiarly raised up...[19]

Iowa Conservatives reported having 241 members in 1878. On the same year they adopted a Book of Discipline and sent epistles "to all sound Friends." [20] Their book of discipline advised on observation of "due moderation" in their housing, the avoidance of "superfluity in their manner of living" and abstention of tobacco as an introduction to what was a return to the simplicity of previous years. They also were concerned about "the solemn duty of pure and spiritual worship," worship "in outward silence rejecting those forms and ceremonies which were invented by the wisdom of man..."[21]

In 1883 a few of them visited Iowa Yearly Meeting of (Conservative) Friends and were given a warm welcome. So, the fourth yearly meeting of Friends in Iowa shortly became three again. Ella Newlin, an older conservative Friend was moved to write many years later in 1945:

> ... It is well they did not foresee the long arduous task that was ahead and the discouragements to be met in the coming years. The sad part was so many of them were aged according to the course of nature. Many of those who feared nothing but being wrong were gathered to their eternal rest we cannot doubt. Numbers were reduced. Some who started out with zeal soon found themselves too weak to bear the cross it involved. Some went back to the big meeting that was then so popular, some quit trying to be anything ... The few young people who dared to go with the elder ones felt it keenly to break away from those who we had mingled with from childhood and the reproach of it all was crushing ... I was convinced of the truth of Friends' principles, in their purity ... Our Savior's teaching was practical common sense religion that applied to every day living ...[22]

14

The 1877 Separation in Plainfield and the 1879 Separation in Kansas

While Indiana Yearly Meeting held together after the Civil War, the rattling and banging in Iowa was echoed in Western Yearly Meeting the same year. Less than twenty years after Western had been set off as an independent yearly meeting they were faced with a schism. The issues were similar to the ones in Iowa: a conservative reaction to evangelicalism and to the new ways of conducting Friends worship:

> For several years prior to 1877 there were introduced into the Society doctrinal teachings and practices which were at variance with the accepted doctrines of the Society ...[1]

Alter a few names of people and places and the rest of the story is similar. In this separation the conservatives in Plainfield Quarter wrote a testimony very like that written at Bear Creek. The quarterly meeting then sent on two reports to Western Yearly Meeting, each claiming to represent Plainfield Quarterly Meeting.[2]

In 1877 Western Yearly Meeting appointed a committee "of men and women to labor for the restoration of the unity of Friends in that meeting."[3] The committee reported back to the Yearly Meeting in 1878. The yearly meeting in turn directed its monthly meetings to "... extend forbearance and Christian care to such of their members as have separated from them, and that there be no discontinuance of membership of them ..."[4] They took a little bit longer, but in 1879 the Yearly Meeting "suggested" the discontinuance of the membership of the adult members who " ... are persisting in holding separate Meetings ..."[5]

The seemingly gentle forbearance of Western Yearly Meeting to its separating members was not quite the same when the events were reported by a visiting English Friend. Several years later Walter Robson wrote to the British Friend describing the break in 1877. He had heard a "venerable Friend of eighty-two" say that he no longer felt he had rights and privileges in the body, and therefore he invited others to withdraw with him. Then, as a large number of Friends put on their hats and left, one of the ministers sang: "See the mighty host advancing, Satan leading on!"[6]

Robson spoke to Western Yearly Meeting later that day on the value of unity among Friends. Some supported these sentiments, while others were "very severe" with him telling him that he was encouraging " ... a spirit they wanted to crush ..." One of the severe Friends was none other than D. B. Updegraff.[7]

The separatists established Western Yearly Meeting of Conservative Friends with two quarterly meetings and several monthly meetings. There was some conflict over property which was eventually settled. The Conservatives then began building new meeting houses and schools. In 1962 after years of decline in membership the Conservative yearly meeting was laid down.[8] Many members rejoined Western Yearly Meeting.

B. Kansas

When Kansas Yearly Meeting was set off from Indiana in 1872, Friends evangelical revival movement was well under way. Kansas, therefore, inherited the discord bedeviling other yearly meetings. As elsewhere, Kansas had a minority strongly against change. Cyrus W. Harvey, a recorded minister and the leader of the conservative group, was active in his opposition to the new movement.[9]

The first attempt to control the evangelicals was made in June, 1879, at Cyrus Harvey's home quarterly meeting. The conservatives tried to get one of their own in as the clerk of the quarter and failed. In a separate gathering after the quarterly meeting Cyrus Harvey was appointed clerk of a Conservative Spring River Quarterly Meeting.[10] That year the minutes of Kansas Yearly Meeting reported:

> The Clerk informs the Meeting that he has received two Reports, each of which purports to come from Spring River Quarterly Meeting. These Reports are referred to the ... representatives for examination, and they are requested to report to our next sitting their

judgment as to which of said Reporters shall be accepted by this Meeting.[11]

A few pages later the Representatives reported as follows:

> ... After due deliberation upon the subject before us, we are united in judgment that the Report signed by John M. Weeks as Clerk is the proper one to be accepted by this Yearly Meeting.[12]

The list of the representatives from Spring River did not include the name of Cyrus Harvey.

By December of that year, Cottonwood Monthly Meeting, of Emporia, was moved to minute:

> On account of the many innovations in our once favored society in regard to our doctrines, principles, practices, we feel necessitated to absent ourselves from those meetings in which these innovations are practiced, that we may maintain our doctrines, principles and practices in the unity of the Spirit in the bond of peace.[13]

The minute was repeated verbatim by the Quarterly Meeting in January, 1880.[14]

At Kansas Yearly Meeting in 1880 notice was given of the withdrawal of twenty-nine families from Cottonwood Quarterly Meeting. Again the yearly meeting appointed a committee to examine the affair. The judgment reported:

> ... subordinate meetings should not at present institute disciplinary proceedings against those who have withdrawn therefrom, on account of said withdrawal, and that in reporting statistics for this meeting, such persons should be included in a separate list of which the meeting approves and directs accordingly."[15]

However, by 1880 it was too late. Conservative Friends had organized their own Kansas Yearly Meeting of Friends with Cyrus Harvey as clerk. Cottonwood became a part of this new yearly meeting, as did a number of other meetings. By 1881, they had set up three quarterly meetings. They corresponded with other conservative yearly meetings and began their own magazine, the *Western Friend.*[16] Then, like their counterparts in Western Yearly Meeting of Conservative Friends in Indiana, these Friends dwindled in numbers. Their yearly meeting was discontinued in 1929. The remaining members joined Iowa Yearly Meeting of Conservative Friends.[17]

15

A Canadian Separation in Two Parts

Friends began to arrive in Upper Canada (now Ontario) shortly after the American Revolution. They established their meetings as extensions of the yearly and quarterly meetings south of the border, just as their counterparts did on the frontier. After 1828 there were Hicksite and Orthodox Friends with established meetings in Upper Canada. In 1867 the British Government granted Canada its political independence, uniting the provinces of Upper and Lower Canada into a new Confederation. At the same time Canada Yearly Meeting was set off by New York Yearly Meeting (O). This action set the stage for the fourth Orthodox yearly meeting division after Ohio, Western, and Kansas Yearly Meetings. Hicksite Friends decided not to set off a separate Canadian yearly meeting, as they saw no need at the time. Instead, Canadian Hicksites remained members of Gennesee Yearly Meeting established several years before in New York State.[1]

The trouble in Canada began in Pelham Quarterly Meeting on the Niagara peninsula. From the time of Confederation to 1877 this quarter was composed of two monthly meetings, Norwich and Pelham, about fifty miles apart. While Pelham Monthly Meeting escaped the worst of the confusion, the first sign of something new appeared in their minutes dated July, 1875. On that day Pelham Monthly Meeting minuted:

> Our beloved Friend William Wetherald, a minister in unity with us feels drawn to Preach the Gospel in Canada, Ohio and New York

121

Yearly Meetings. Full unity being expressed with him in his concern he is left at liberty to pursue his prospects earnestly desiring that the Lord may be his helper.[2]

It was the first time somebody was given leave to "Preach the Gospel" by Pelham. In spite of its innovation, Pelham continued to lead a peaceful life. People were received into membership, a high proportion of whom were women. Nobody was disowned — quite unlike Norwich — and no mention was made of any troubles elsewhere. Another sign of a difference came January 1, 1879, when Pelham Monthly Meeting of Men and Women Friends began holding joint sessions. This was a return to the form that existed before George Fox set up the separate women's meetings in the seventeenth century.[3] It was an indication of reduced membership that made holding separate meetings impractical.

Norwich Monthly meeting's minutes did not have the peaceful tone of Pelham's. During the 1860s they recorded a fairly high number of people who " ... had so far deviated from the order and discipline of our Society ..." as to require having elders " ... appointed to visit them thereon and report..." back to the Meeting. By the early 1870s the frequency of these minutes was reduced to be replaced with minutes welcoming people into membership. In 1876 Norwich Monthly Meeting was able to report and minute the facts that during the past year " ... 15 (were) received into membership — no resignations. None disowned."[4] As in Pelham, a surprisingly high proportion of the new members were young women.

The feeling of triumph in such minutes was soon lost. By October the only thing Norwich Friends could agree on was to adjourn to meet the following month.[5] In November, as was normal, they answered the Queries. This let them prepare their report to the Quarterly Meeting. Their answer to the second query described part of their problem. It read in part:

Ans. 2. There is a lack of Christian love amongst us, arising from a want of unity of sentiment ... [6]

Having answered the queries they conducted no more business. Norwich Monthly Meeting adjourned to meet again the following week. The second meeting was no better, so they reported:

The meeting was so divided in sentiment as to be incapable of transacting the business claiming its attention according to our order and Discipline. Therefore it was adjourned to the usual time next

122

month."[7]

Things went a little better in December. Their representatives reported on the actions of quarterly meeting. They agreed to accept Mary Jane Cohoe, Elizabeth Walker, Almira Adelle Jeffry, and Elizabeth Smith into membership and rejected Luisa Charlotte Nicholson. All other business was deferred.[8] The new year brought no agreement on anything except an approval for a couple to marry. By then a concerned quarterly meeting sent Norwich the following letter:

> The Meeting was introduced into a deep concern on account of there being no official account of Norwich Monthly Meeting, which resulted in appointing the following Friends as a committee of inquiry; with instructions to render such service and advice as they may deem best; and to report their judgment thereon to our next Quarterly Meeting: viz. Squire W. Hill, Andrew Hill, Elisha Taylor, Jacob Gainer, Jr., John Richard Harris, Alfred R. Spencer, Samuel Hill, Job R. Moore and Wm. Spencer.[9]

Norwich Monthly Meeting did no business other than approving a marriage and a certificate of removal. "The subject before the meeting" was the holding of "indulged meetings." These were the same as the general meetings already being held in the American Midwest. Some Norwich Friends had written asking to be allowed to hold indulged meetings, much to the disapproval of other Friends. The Quarterly Meeting wrote a reply which came in time for their March, 1877, monthly meeting:

> Dear Friends: The Committee appointed by Pelham Quarterly Meeting to visit Norwich Monthly Meeting find on examination no clause in the Book of Discipline for Indulged Meetings — But each Established Meeting for worship, should be a Preparative Meeting except in cases where the Quarterly Meeting should judge it inexpedient (Book of Discipline, page 30) which to us seems imperative on the part of the Monthly Meeting to observe the Clause of Discipline on this subject ... [10]

The letter was signed by Squire W. Hill.

Norwich conservatives were quite happy to get the quarterly meeting answer. What was being rejected was something they had not wanted for themselves. At the June monthly meeting the Norwich Friends recorded receiving the letter. They failed to read the queries and appoint representatives to quarterly meeting as they should have.

123

They also welcomed visitors from Michigan and Ireland. It is probably significant that the two visitors from Indiana who had been made welcome by Pelham Quarterly Meeting of Women Friends held three days later were not present at monthly meeting.[11] Having partisan visitors there did nothing to prevent unseemly behavior.

The summer months of 1877 saw no business transacted and no agreement on the appointment of Clerks and overseers at Norwich. In August Pelham Quarterly Meeting, having received no report from Norwich, appointed an investigation committee. That committee reported back in September to the effect:

> ... that the true record of the meeting of seventh month had not been made in regard to appointing a committee to bring forward names for clerks and overseers, which the committee claimed should be recognized by said monthly meeting, after considerable opposition the clerk and a portion of the Friends withdrew contrary to the wishes of the larger portion of the Meeting and the Quarterly Meeting's Committee.[12]

They went on to report that Michael Gillam was appointed clerk. Pelham Quarterly Meeting, therefore, recommended that all the documents signed by him should be considered the legal documents of Norwich Monthly Meeting.

Minutes of Norwich Monthly Meeting, now exclusively composed of conservatives, described the events in quite a different way. Their report says that the name of Michael Gillam was strongly objected to by several, and it was then dropped.[13] No further business was transacted that day. A month later they reported there was "no unity in the proceedings."[14] By September, however, the evangelicals had withdrawn into their own monthly meeting, also called Norwich Monthly Meeting. After that the two sides refused to accept each other's minutes. They both began the process of removing each other from membership. Adam Spencer remained active in the branch now labeled Conservative. The conservatives were able to proceed with what was seen as normal procedures when they appointed representatives to quarterly meeting and read the queries. Jesse Stover, Wm. B. Mason, John Sutton and Adam Spencer were asked to take their answers, which included:

> Ans. 2. There is such a lack of Christian love amongst us, arising from differences of sentiments that we have not been able to transact the business of the meeting.[15]

Two weeks later Norwich Monthly Meeting (C) reconvened. Their representatives returned to report to quarterly meeting that:

> Friends were exercised at this time under a humbling sense of the sorrowful state of things amongst us, and of the difficulties of our present situation ...

As a consequence Norwich appointed a committee to:

> ... take into serious consideration the propriety of our issuing a Testimony or Declaration concerning the separation from us of a portion of the members of this meeting ...[16]

At Pelham Quarterly Meeting (C) held on the 15th of 9th month, 1877, a new minute book appeared. (The old minute book was in the hands of the Orthodox). The new minute book's first entry records the presence of representatives from Norwich and the absence of any from Pelham because "that meeting having identified itself with those who have separated from Norwich Monthly Meeting."[17] They appointed Adam Spencer for clerk and William B. Stover for assistant. They recognized the " ... lack of Christian love" answer to the second query and the "disturbed state of Society ..." in answer to the 9 th query. The disturbed sense of the Society and the lack of Christian love exercised them several times later that year and early in 1878. Quarterly Meeting kept on reporting the absence of representatives from Pelham and the concern that " ... talebearing not altogether avoided and discouraged ..."[18]

In June, 1878, it came time to appoint representatives to yearly meeting, answer the queries and write their report to the yearly meeting. For their report both sides described what had taken place the previous September. The reports from two Pelham quarterly meetings were sent on to Canada Yearly Meeting held in 1878. One set was signed by Adam Spencer for the conservatives and the other signed by John R. Harris for the Orthodox.

The yearly meeting committee appointed to investigate the matter recommended that the report signed by John R. Harris be received. At this point Adam Spencer stood, and said he no longer considered himself to be a member of Canada Yearly meeting, and left. There were twenty-five visitors to that yearly meeting, the majority of whom were representatives from the American Midwest.[19] They helped outnumber Norwich's conservatives.

News of this break was received by conservative groups elsewhere. In November, 1879, the quarterly meeting (C) reported having received a letter from Western Yearly Meeting (C). In June, 1880, they received a letter from Spring River Quarterly Meeting of Friends in Kansas that was in answer to the one they had sent in September, 1879. With this kind of satisfaction, they began to correspond with conservative Friends in other parts of North America.

One of the issues bothering Adam Spencer and his conservative allies was the revision of the new Discipline which had been adopted two years earlier in 1877 by New York Yearly Meeting. As Canada was its daughter meeting, the expectation was that the same would happen with little discussion in Canada. This Discipline changed some wording, which Arthur Dorland, the well-known Canadian historian, and member of an Orthodox meeting, found was not "radical."[20] The new Discipline omitted reference to "plainness of dress," the provision against "hireling ministry" and the acceptance of money by a minister of the gospel. These were central to the discomfort felt by other conservative Friends and were troublesome to the Canadians. The new Discipline was to limit the time of service of elders to "a period of three years," a matter clearly aimed at the older conservative members.

The new Discipline was discussed at yearly meeting in Pickering in 1880 by Representative Meeting. They formally recommended that the New York Discipline of 1877 be adopted as the Discipline of Canada Yearly Meeting of Friends. There is no evidence in the minutes that there was any opposition to this move. The yearly meeting also decided to cooperate in the work of the American Friends Foreign Missionary Board.[21]

The revised Discipline was sent on for adoption by the quarterly meetings and again became the focus of disagreement. Conservative Friends who were upset but still within the yearly meeting began to correspond with their counterparts in Norwich. In 1881 the conservatives in Westlake Monthly and Quarterly Meetings withdrew from the yearly meeting. These Friends invited the Friends in Norwich: " ... to hold Canada Yearly Meeting at Pickering at the appointed time ..." [22] This, in effect, was the beginning of Canada Yearly Meeting Conservative.

16

The 1902-1905 Division in North Carolina

The four divisions in Western, Kansas, Iowa and Canada Yearly Meetings were a shock to the Society of Friends everywhere. North Carolina Friends were linked to factions on both sides through bonds of family, friendship and visits in the ministry. North Carolina Friends had the same debates, and said very much the same sort of things in those debates. Yet, North Carolina Friends did not divide at the time.

Friends in North Carolina were proud of being part of a yearly meeting that had never divided. They had been at considerable risk in 1846 when two epistles had arrived from New England. Nathan Hunt had saved them that time. This widely respected elder was the father of Thomas Hunt, the clerk of the yearly meeting. He objected to reading the Wilburite epistle and persuaded Friends to read the Gurneyite epistle that day. Allen Jay, therefore, credits him with preventing a division.[1]

In the late 1870s the possibility of a division was also present in North Carolina. The issues were like those in the Midwest and in Canada. Rich Square Monthly Meeting Friends, for example, were quite opposed to the whole evangelical movement. They consistently refused to pay the portion of the yearly meeting's assessment for evangelism after 1874.[2] Further, these Friends were in regular contact with other conservative yearly meetings.[3]

Evangelism was a contentious matter for many years. However, it was not until 1890, sixteen years later, that the yearly meeting relented and excused Friends with scruples from paying their full assessment. Rich Square Friends and others were relieved by this. However, the action irritated Friends in other meetings. Six years later the yearly meeting reversed itself to insist that Eastern Quarter pay its full assessment.[4] Another six years were to pass before North Carolina Yearly Meeting divided into Orthodox and Conservative yearly meetings. This was three decades after the beginning of the evangelical revivals organized by Allen Jay and almost as long after the refusal of Rich Square Friends to pay their full assessment.

The explanation offered by Damon Hickey for the division is that sectional rivalries, economic differences, the evangelistic movement, the organizational changes introduced by this movement, and the desire to preserve traditional Friends distinctiveness, combined to produce the separation.[5] The explanation leaves unanswered the question of why North Carolina failed to divide at the time the other yearly meetings divided. The issues were the same, yet North Carolina waited another twenty-five years.

The reason for North Carolina's delay can probably be found in their experience during and after the Civil War. During the Civil War North Carolina Friends, for the most part, stood by their testimony against war. They were persecuted and suffered for their principles. Some members had escaped by migrating to the Midwest. Others obtained release when they went to work producing salt for the Confederacy. Salt production was one of the very few un-warlike things Friends could do to avoid being dragged into the army. Those who did not escape or work on salt production were treated brutally and forced into the army. Several lost their lives from the mistreatment they were given. Three Friends forced to fight for the Confederacy were taken prisoners by the North during a battle but were released into Friends custody by President Lincoln. Lincoln, unlike Davis, was sympathetic towards the Friends peace testimony.[6]

Friends had migrated from North Carolina to Indiana in large numbers before the war. Some managed to get away during the war. Many returned to North Carolina after the war was over to rebuild. They combined efforts with Friends from the North and Midwest in the work of the Baltimore Association of Friends. This organization was set up first under the direction of Joseph Moore and then under Allen Jay, both from Indiana, to advise and assist Friends in the Southern States. It was founded by wealthy Friends in Baltimore to provide the basic help in surviving. It began a series of educational and production experiments that greatly enhanced the lives of the people in war devastated areas. Much of the work was later taken over by state institutions. Midwestern Friends had the skills, knowledge and experience to aid and, therefore, contributed some of the most influential people to the Association.[7]

Like Midwestern Friends, North Carolina Friends had been influenced by pre-war revivals beginning in the 1850s. Evangelicalism spread in North Carolina Yearly Meeting after the war when Midwestern Friends brought it with them.[8] North Carolina Friends welcomed them with open arms. The Friends coming to help were the young, active and religiously dedicated people. They had been affected by the the religious changes at home and now wanted to help rebuild in a new and better way.

Like their counterparts in the Midwest, it was the young North Carolina Friends who were first captivated by the new religious ideas. They led the way, with older Friends objecting strenuously, as they had in the Midwest. In North Carolina there was an important difference. Allen Jay was there as Superintendent of Education for the Baltimore Association. He was also one of the evangelicals who had been instrumental in the changes in Indiana. By combining the legitimacy of his position and his religious feelings he was able to reconcile the differences between the older and younger Friends.[9] In this he only did what he had already done in Indiana.

The young Friends desire for evangelical prayer meetings reached the floor of North Carolina Yearly Meeting in 1870. They appointed a Committee on General Meetings, following the Midwestern model, with no record of any objection. Allen Jay, who had brought the idea with him and probably proposed it, was the first person appointed to this new committee.[10] The form of General Meetings and the precedent of their use in Indiana made the activities legitimate for the entire yearly meeting. These meetings were held at other than the normal times of worship, providing a new pattern of worship to Friends.[11]

In 1872, the Committee appointed to hold General Meetings reported they had held five meetings:

> ... all of which we believe were owned by the Head of the Church and were favored seasons, which has been the means of spreading a knowledge of our principles amongst others, and highly appreciated by many and we believe that a wide door is opened for further labor in that direction.[12]

Allen Jay left North Carolina in 1872 after "turning over his responsibilities to the yearly meeting."[13]

In 1874 Rich Square Friends refused to pay their full assessment to the yearly meeting. They began traveling in the ministry and by 1879 were in contact with the newly separated conservative yearly meet-

129

ings. Eastern Quarter Friends admitted to a "low degree of life in our Religious Meetings."[14] They received support for their opposition to evangelicalism from Friends in Philadelphia and from the conservative yearly meetings. However, in spite of the activity in Iowa, Western, Kansas and Canada Yearly Meetings, no break occurred at this time.

In 1882, the General Meetings Committee became the Evangelistic Committee. "At the same yearly meeting session, the first formal contact ... with other denominations was announced."[15] In 1883 Eastern Quarter began to discuss the possibility of withdrawing from North Carolina Yearly Meeting and joining Baltimore Yearly Meeting. However, they rejected the idea at the time.[16]

North Carolina Yearly Meeting sent representatives to the Conferences of Friends in 1887 and in 1892. After the second conference, the Discipline Committee proposed the acceptance of " ... the Declaration of Faith issued by the Richmond conference in 1887"[17] to the yearly meeting in 1893. There were objections from Rich Square Monthly Meeting and Eastern Quarter to this change in the Discipline.[18] In spite of the objections, the yearly meeting went ahead with the printing and distribution of the new Disciplines.[19]

In 1896, the yearly meeting again tried to persuade Eastern Quarter to pay its entire assessment. Friends in Eastern Quarter had consistently continued to refuse to pay their part of the cost of evangelistic work.[20] In 1898, Eastern Quarter set out their objections to the yearly meeting's evangelistic practices:

> ... This ... has led into such departures as hired ministry, congregational singing, instrumental music, pre-arranged 'prayer meetings', testimony meetings, & etc ... [We] are persuaded that such ... can only tend to lead us farther and farther from the desired unity of faith and practice ...[21]

Their objections could have come from the minutes of any of the conservative groups in Indiana, Iowa, Kansas or Canada from twenty years before.

To defuse the conflict, the yearly meeting that year appropriated nothing for evangelism, but instead they made an:[22]

> ... appeal to Friends for voluntary contributions for the support of the work, with the prayer that the hearts of our membership may be united in the support of the hands of the Committee for the ensuing year ... [23]

In 1900, two years later, the issue was back in full force. The

Evangelistic Committee made an accounting of money spent. They asked for twenty-five dollars from each meeting to be raised by assessment to cover its expenses.[24] Their report showed they had spent thrity-four dollars in the Eastern Quarter. The name of the committee was changed again in 1900 to become the Home Missions Committee.

North Carolina Yearly Meeting had also been discussing the proposal for accepting the "The Constitution and Discipline of the American Yearly Meetings of Friends" commonly called the Uniform Discipline, but no final action was taken that year.[25] In 1901 the matter was taken up, and again they laid it over for the next yearly meeting. Finally, after further consideration in its sessions in 1902, the yearly meeting adopted the Uniform Discipline over the objections of Eastern Quarterly Meeting.[26] A significant aspect of the new Discipline was the ultimate authority given to the yearly meeting over individual meetings.

Thirty years of evangelical-revivalistic activity had changed the nature of the worship for many Friends. The young Friends of the 1870s had become elders in their own meetings and in the yearly meeting. They felt that the Richmond Conferences showed Friends at their best, working together in a corporate way for common goals. To them the Richmond Declaration of Faith and Uniform Discipline were valuable products of this work. The separated Hicksites and Conservatives were no longer regarded as Friends. Therefore, Friends who echoed them, such as Rich Square Friends, could safely be ignored. Even though the Conservatives stood for "ancient practice," they were standing in the way of progress. Most Friends in North Carolina wanted to move ahead with the larger bodies of Friends elsewhere, especially those in the Midwest.

The view of the Conservative Friends was different. They felt that Friends traditional testimonies were being violated. They claimed that their testimony against a "hireling ministry" raised questions that were never given an adequate hearing, that paying an evangelist or a minister was simply wrong, and that the music and prearranged worship that accompanied these departures were also contrary to ancient testimonies. Then, The Richmond Declaration of Faith, a statement bordering on being credal, was imposed on them by the yearly meeting. The new Discipline, which was also imposed on them, changed the relationship between monthly and yearly meeting giving the yearly meeting new powers: " ... to decide all questions of administration; to counsel, admonish or discipline its subordinate meetings ..." [27] From the point of view of conservative Friends, this was the final blow.

The effect of the adoption of the Uniform Discipline on the Friends in the Eastern Quarter soon became evident. Eastern Quarterly Meeting did not send delegates to the 1903 North Carolina Yearly Meeting. Their absence was noted and their difficulties were discussed. The yearly meeting named a committee "labor therein," that is, to try to persuade them to change their views.[28] In 1904 the committee reported its failure to bring about a reconciliation. Eastern Quarter Friends did not send delegates to yearly meeting that year.[29] Their absence and their refusal to pay yearly meeting assessments for evangelism showed that the differences had become insurmountable. In fact, the committee's report of failure to achieve reconciliation was acknowledgment of a division.

Although feelings were hurt by the separation, and there was some anger and righteous indignation on both sides, the division was remarkably peaceful when compared to other divisions. For example, Algie Newlin described how his parents and brother withdrew from the evangelical meeting to form a conservative one on "ancient principles." He eventually became clerk of the North Carolina Yearly Meeting while, at the same time, his brother became clerk of the Conservative yearly meeting. When this occurred there was speculation of having the two yearly meetings rejoin, but that did not happen. Families that divided over the yearly meeting issues maintained cordial relations. The Conservatives in Rich Square, however, did go through a pro-forma disownment procedure for those who chose to separate from them.[30]

The major issues were very like those in Iowa, Kansas, Western and Canada Yearly Meetings. In them the majority of the young people, reinforced by some older Friends, became enamored with the ideas of the evangelical revivals. Disapproval was usually general at first. As the pioneers received outside legitimation, and as they were joined by significant numbers they eventually prevailed. The early ministers in these movements were usually young and often female. However, as the movements gathered strength and became institutionalized, the young became older and the women ceased to hold their importance. Now, where their descendants worship, worship is infrequently led by women or by young people.

The question of why it took North Carolina Friends so long to go through their neo-conservative division can by answered by their war-time and immediate post-war experiences. They suffered far more than any Midwestern group of Friends did during the Civil War. Once the war was over, their common suffering and the effort to rebuild united them.

New evangelical ideas and practices came with the help from the Baltimore Association. Allen Jay as Superintendent of Education and as an evangelical minister embodied both. Older Friends were faced with the dilemma of new and unpalatable ideas carried by a person who was doing a lot to help them. They could not accept the help on the one hand and refuse the ideas on the other. Their disagreement was muted but did not disappear. Jay's departure in 1872 let the conservatives begin to express their disagreement, but it did not provide time enough to divide them when the other yearly meetings divided. Instead, the objectors looked for other ways to express their disapproval. One group, Rich Square Friends, simply refused to pay their part of the assessment for evangelism.

The call to meet at Richmond in 1887 attracted those who were most like Midwestern Friends. The Declaration of Faith and the Uniform Discipline became theirs as it fitted in so nicely with their evangelicalism. Their sense of ownership, combined with the legitimacy provided by the larger gathering, reinforced their convictions about the no longer so new forms of worship. Their return to Richmond five years later gave them a renewed conviction that they were right. The Uniform Discipline also gave them the power to enforce these ideas on the conservatives.

The Conservatives now no longer got help from the Baltimore Association. They had made contact with other conservative Friends who shared their views. The contact freed them to react to a statement of faith that looked like a creed and to a new Discipline that took away their autonomy. When both the creed and the new Discipline were imposed on them, a practice also contrary to Friends traditions, North Carolina Yearly Meeting divided just as the others had twenty-five years earlier. The division came over a new manifestation of the same old issues.

The matter of property was settled peacefully, with Conservative Friends keeping the larger meeting house at Cedar Grove, while the others kept the smaller one at Rich Square. There followed a series of smaller withdrawals in various parts of the state. The separating Friends came together shortly after to form North Carolina Yearly Meeting (Conservative).

17

Central Yearly Meeting

Of all the yearly meetings in North America probably the least well known is Central Yearly Meeting. This small yearly meeting, composed mainly of rural, small town, laboring people, came into existence in a separation from Western Yearly Meeting in 1924. The story is bound up with the creation of a public education system in the State of Indiana and with the Friends School in Westfield.

Union High Academy had been created under the care of the Westfield Monthly Meeting in the village of Westfield in 1861. In November 1879, the school was deeded to the Union High School Associates, who served as its board of directors and who reported once a year to the monthly meeting. By 1911 it had become obvious that the school could no longer serve the purpose for which it had been established. The State of Indiana had established a system of free public education, and the system drew off many of the students Union High had, making it impractical as a Quaker academy. It then became the Union Bible Seminary under the direction of William M. Smith.[1]

William M. Smith's goal was that the Seminary be a place where ministers and missionaries could be trained for service. Smith was a man described by Harold Tollefson as a brilliant Bible scholar with tremendous magnetism.[2] Smith was a strong advocate of the Richmond Declaration of Faith and of George Fox's letter to the governor of Barbadoes, and he was quite certain about biblical inerrancy. He was, therefore, very opposed to new ideas in science, particularly biology, philosophy and religion. By 1919 there were enough graduates from the seminary that the first missionaries were sent out by Western and Indiana Yearly Meetings. By then, too, several more had begun serving as pastors in Indiana and Ohio.

In contrast to the rigid religious training at Union Bible Seminary, new ideas in science, philosophy, biology and religion were affecting the curricula in many colleges and universities, among them Earlham College. As early as 1912, recently graduated seminarians from Union Bible Seminary and others who shared William Smith's views had written letters to Earlham complaining about Elbert Russell's teaching of the scientific explanation of biblical accounts.[3] Moreover, according to their accounts, Earlham students were also experimenting with new styles of dress and had taken up card playing and smoking. These accusations, added to the criticisms already made, further disturbed Friends.

This developed into an open controversy at Indiana Yearly Meeting in 1920 when Portland Quarterly Meeting came with:

> ... a deep concern about the conditions of our Church ... caused by the many conflicting reports ... about certain teaching and methods among us ... requested an examination of the Five Years Meeting, Earlham Seminary and the *American Friend.*[4]

At the time most of the pastors in Portland Quarter were recent graduates of Union Bible Seminary.[5]

This concern, combined with a similar one raised at Western Yearly Meeting, led to the formation of a joint committee to investigate Earlham College. The committee, as it happened, was composed of Friends who were sympathetic to Earlham. They were asked to report to the Earlham Board of Trustees, who in turn report back to the two yearly meetings.

A full report of the committee's investigation was published in the April, 1921, issue of the Earlham College Bulletin. The central conclusion was that the differences between the complainants and the college were due largely to differences in phraseology or to questions:

> ... which involve only technical theological definitions, and which do not endanger any vital spiritual doctrine, or the credibility of the Scriptures.[6]

Just before the issue of the *Bulletin* appeared, but after the report had been made to the College's Board of Trustees, a "group of ten," all with ties to Union Bible Seminary but not all from Portland Quarter, publicly reiterated their objections. This took the form of a "Letter to Friends of Indiana Yearly Meeting" and it was followed quickly by "An Appeal to the Membership of Indiana Yearly Meeting." They objected to the way Earlham taught Bible, philosophy, and psychology. They felt the report to the Board plastered over differences that were far deeper than suggested.[7] Their real objections were best phrased in the "Appeal":

> The real controversy centers around this — shall the Church control and correct the College, or shall the College be allowed to control the Church and blast away the foundation stones of its Declaration of Faith. The Evidence of the Committee of Ten and the admission of the Faculty of Earlham show that they teach EVOLUTION, and make IT the basis of their interpretation of the Bible. The belief in this unscientific and unproven Evolutionary Theory' compels them to ... admit there are parts of the Bible that they do not believe ...[8]

However, Portland Quarterly Meeting also had another objective in view. It requested Western and Indiana Yearly Meetings accept the Richmond Declaration as a creed[9] and it proposed to persuade all other yearly meetings in the Five Years Meeting to do the same. In order to accomplish this goal it asked Indiana Yearly Meeting to rescind its action taken in 1912 by omitting the phrase "... but they are not to be regarded as constituting a creed ..."[10] However, the Permanent Board of the yearly meeting refused to endorse this concern,[11] confirming the decision taken by the Conference of Friends in 1887.[12]

At the Five Years Meeting in 1922, with support from Kansas and Oregon Yearly Meetings, Portland Q. M. again raised this issue.[13] Other yearly meetings, however, objected referring to Friends long standing testimony against creeds as the basis for their rejection of this proposal. The Business Committee's response, presented by Rufus M. Jones, tried to balance the desires of both groups and replied with a minute that read:

> We recognize with profound sorrow that there is in the world today a great drift of religious unsettlement unconcern and unbelief. We desire at this time to call our own membership to a deeper religious life, a greater consecration of heart and will to God and a more positive loyalty to the faith from which so many of our forerunners suffered and died. We wish to reaffirm the statements and declaration of faith contained in our Uniform Discipline, vis,

The Essential Truths, 'Declaration of Faith' issued by the Richmond Conference in 1887 and 'George Fox's Letter to the Governor of Barbadoes'...[14]

To soften the impact of this on the people who wanted change they further recommended that:

> ... this meeting instruct its Publication Board to issue in attractive form an edition of these three documents as the authorized Declaration of Faith of the Five Years Meeting of Friends in America ...[15]

Thus they "reaffirmed" the statements but did not transform them into a creed.

William M. Smith the founder and director of Union Bible Seminary and editor of the *Gospel Minister,* who had been pivotal in presenting the objections to yearly meeting, now faced defeat on issues central to his beliefs. He thundered out in editorials and lead articles in the *Gospel Minister.* He had founded and edited this paper to serve as an adjunct to the teaching at the seminary. He was particularly irritated by the nature of the financial support of Earlham College and the fact that by his membership in the local meeting he was forced to support the college. The membership financial quota included a portion that went to the support of the college. He could see no way to escape paying for something he thoroughly disapproved of, so he resigned his membership in the Society of Friends.[16]

Then, in February, 1924, in the words of Harold Tollefson, who with other students from the Seminary witnessed it:

> I was teaching Church History in the high school division of the Seminary [Union Bible Seminary]. J. Edwin Newby, Principal of the high school section, came into the room that morning and announced: 'We are not going to study Church History today. We are going over to Quarterly Meeting and either transfer our membership to Ohio Yearly Meeting (Damascus) or start our own Quarterly Meeting.' Then he led the student body over to the Meeting house where they sat as a body. The Seminary students, mostly adults, were already there. William Smith was not present as he was no longer a member of the Westfield Meeting.

Richard R. Newby was the speaker that morning and gave a powerful message. During the business session Paton Cox arose and asked that his membership be transferred to Gillead Monthly Meeting in Ohio Yearly Meeting. There was a brief silence, and then Mahlon Day, of Westfield, stood and read a section from the Western Yearly

Meeting Discipline. It dealt with membership and stated simply that membership must be placed where the person has his residence.

> The clerk then announced that the request of Paton Cox could not be granted. This Friend ... then stated clearly: 'If I can not have my membership transferred then I shall withdraw and form my own monthly meeting, and anyone in this room is invited to join me.' He then walked out the door and was followed by the entire seminary group.[17]

The desire to join Ohio Yearly Meeting came in part from the link the Seminary had established through the graduates working in Ohio. Ohio Yearly Meeting was even more attractive to them because it had gone through an evangelical transformation.[18] Therefore William Smith and others on his side in Westfield Meeting felt Ohio Yearly Meeting was more congenial than either Western or Indiana Yearly Meetings were at the time especially since Ohio Yearly Meeting did not form a part of the Five Years Meeting and did not have a link with Earlham College or with the *American Friend.*

The withdrawal in Westfield was followed by others: Fort Wayne on November 22nd., Bethany on March 21, 1925, then by Number Eleven, Randolph, Alexandria, Wayne County, Dunkirk and several others.[19] Union Quarterly Meeting was formed in 1924, and on September 17, 1926 these meetings came together to create Central Yearly Meeting with its own Discipline, organization and mission program.[20]

This separation differs in interesting ways from the earlier separations in Iowa, Western, Kansas, Canada and North Carolina Yearly Meetings. Those were divisions between people who wanted to retain their ancient conservative ways and people who were working actively to introduce ideas and practices that fit their new evangelical ideas. The withdrawal of Central Yearly Meeting Friends was also of a small, homogeneous group that objected to new ideas. In this division there were three contentious issues under discussion. They were issues on which Smith and his followers had found unity. Two of them were their opposition to the teaching of evolution and the new philosophical and critical interpretation of the Bible at Earlham College. Their objection included recognition that these ideas also affected the content of the *American Friend.* Other Friends in Western and Indiana Yearly Meetings agreed with them on these ideas, but did not isolate themselves from the college and the journal.

The third issue separating Central Friends from others was not of the same order. In their struggle over the first two ideas Central

138

Friends had perceived a threat to their faith. To purify the Society of Friends, they demanded the transformation of the Richmond Declaration of Faith into a creed. This demand ran counter to Friends traditional opposition to credal statements and further separated them from potential allies in both yearly meetings.

William Smith's ideas remained relatively unchanged on these issues from the time he founded Union Bible Seminary. He found kindred spirits and support from others who worked with him and from the students who graduated. While he was building his group, the faculty at Earlham College was teaching the new ideas. Smith's awareness of this caused him to begin his campaign to bring about a change. The campaign went through several stages, culminating in the trial and decision of the Five Years Meeting to reaffirm the Declaration of Faith. By then enough time had elapsed for a new generation to realize how different they were from the main body of Friends and, although the division was emotional, it had a sense of inevitability about it. It was almost as if everybody was relieved it had taken place and that it was quite useless to try to avoid it.

Central Friends made no appeal to "ancient traditions" nor to long-standing practices. Instead they argued against the new and for a retention and strengthening of what had come to be important to their faith. While their tactics and rhetoric may have been different, the result was similar to that achieved in earlier conservative divisions: preservation of what was perceived as important. After the break they simply went ahead and formed their new yearly meeting as they wanted it to be. And, like some Conservative Friends, they have not formed alliances with other yearly meetings.

Central Yearly Meeting is characterized by the pastoral, evangelistic, holiness tradition of some other yearly meetings. It has isolated itself from much of late twentieth century life, holding to strict moral codes for dress and behavior and shunning public entertainment and media. Central Yearly Meeting has had very little contact with other groups of Friends, so little contact that in an interview with several of their members in December 1979, one of them reported that the Evangelical Friends Alliance " ... never got off the ground ..." Their main contact is with Northwest Yearly Meeting, primarily through their common interest in mission work in Bolivia. Some of the graduates of the seminary have found pulpits in other yearly meetings, but even there the mutual interchange of information does not seem to have affected Central Yearly Meeting Friends. They have tended to carry on their activities in social isolation, making as few compromises as possible when working with others. The membership is small, and their intense mission program in Bolivia has a budget that exceeds that of the yearly meeting by a large margin.[21]

Central Yearly Meeting Friends patterns of worship, language, and basic ideas closely resemble those of other rural Indiana Yearly Meeting Friends. The rural isolation of both groups appears to have had a homogenizing effect on them as the differences are surprisingly small. Central Friends have Union Bible Seminary, while Indiana Friends have the Earlham School of Religion at Earlham College. My impression was that the link between rural Friends and Union Bible Seminary is more congenial than it is to the Earlham School of Religion. The differences between the two schools is immense, from almost any point of view. Yet, a Central Friend who accidentally arrived at the door of a rural meeting belonging to Indiana Yearly Meeting would feel at home.

Central Friends isolation is a self-imposed isolation that I find to be rather sad. Their similarity to other Indiana Friends and to many in the Evangelical Friends Alliance is striking. Theologically they would fit very comfortably within the continuum found in EFA's fundamental, evangelical, holiness tradition. One can hope, perhaps, that such a link might be formed some day.

The rules published for controlling the behavior of students and staff of Union Bible Seminary are rigid in their extreme. They proscribe every form of modern entertainment and insist on a victorian modesty of dress. (Skirts and stockings have to leave no bare skin exposed, sleeves are to come to the wrist, no jewelry is permitted, and women's hair should remain uncut. Men are not to wear shorts or have short sleeves.) The rules that govern the contact between unmarried people of the opposite sex are equally rigid. Dates, for example, are limited to one per month, lasting for a half hour and then only in the presence of the Dean or other staff member.

The Seminary is a curiously anachronistic institution, one that combines nineteenth century features with some relatively modern equipment. The physical plant of the Seminary, when I visited it in December 1979, had a museum quality about it, as though it were frozen in time and preserved for modern visitors. They have a working linotype press that is used to publish the *Gospel Minister*, their books and pamphlets. Their classrooms, meeting room and bookstore all have the same atmosphere.

Both Portland Quarterly Meeting and Westfield Monthly Meeting reported little change in membership during the period of the division. The former showed an increase in its members between

1923 and 1925, and further growth was reported in subsequent years when it became Van Wert Regional Meeting.

There was one final twist to this separation: William Smith bought the Union Bible Seminary property from the Union High School Association. The money he paid was passed on by Westfield Monthly Meeting through Western Yearly Meeting, and consequently, a portion went to Earlham College. Westfield established a scholarship for Friends students from their quarterly meeting who attend Earlham. Smith made payments in 1933, 1939 and the last one in 1943 when he finally obtained a clear title to the Seminary property. In effect, William Smith has helped pay for a scholarship for students to study at Earlham.

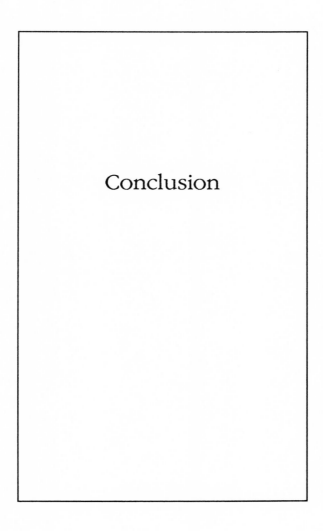

Conclusion

Friends long history of work for the sake of peace is not put into question by the findings of this book. Their refusal to serve in armed forces, and their work with refugees and in ambulance corps during wartime is evidence of their sincerity. It is strange, therefore, to find times when these peace-loving people divided into warring factions and came to blows over their beliefs. The chapters above only provide an indication of how difficult it is to avoid conflict. They also give insight into how conflict can come about.

Friends very strong feeling about consensus makes these internal conflicts more difficult to understand. In Quaker business meetings before proceeding with a decision, the members look for agreement. The importance of agreement is shown by the many ways Friends have of expressing it: seeking unity, seeking the sense of the meeting, waiting in the Light, obeying the will of God, listening to the Inward Light. Yet it is obvious that Friends do disagree, and they have disagreed quite often.

Lack of agreement on important matters is not unusual in any group of people. However, disagreement among Friends has seldom been enough to break links between friends and relatives. Most of the time Friends, again like others, can disagree on some matters and agree on others. They then may simply agree to disagree and carry on with the normal existence. A lack of agreement is not often strong enough to produce anger. Even less frequently is there enough anger to descend to mild physical violence. This is as far as any Friend has gone, which is not bad for more than three and a half centuries of debate.

When anger does come, it shows itself in curious ways. One of the angriest statements I have ever heard one Friend say to another was said by a girl to her younger brother. She was absolutely livid at the time. She said :"Thee's a little YOU, thee is!" I have also seen Friends walk out of meeting with tears in their eyes over a disagreement. This did not keep the angry person from going back a month later to discuss it over again. I have seen Friends do this on the same important matter for years on end and maintain cordial relations in other matters.

The question raised by this book is not why anger is created but why it becomes great enough to disrupt relations. When I began to work on this topic I wanted to see if it was possible to avoid conflict and the hurt that comes from it. Although pain is one product of conflict, conflict can be a creative and adaptive process. Without conflict, Friends would not have the variety of worship and belief they now have.

Conflict has led to divisions and produced separate branches of the Religious Society of Friends. Each branch has then grown and changed in its own way. As groups have developed, they have become less like each other than they were at the time they divided. At the same time some have come to share forms of worship and beliefs that make them more like other denominations.

The marvelously creative differences would not have come about without disagreement. People who have been attracted into the Society might not have become members without this variety, and there would be fewer Friends. Yet, the pain of conflict has also driven Friends to other churches.

A. Heresy

Looking at history from the point of view of creative religious disagreement includes both the problems of heresy and sacrilege, i. e., violations of belief and religiously unacceptable behavior. Heresy can only be committed by people who are believers within a particular religious body. They are "...close enough to be threatening but distant enough to be considered in error..."[1] Heresy by a non-believer is only a reflection of non-belief. To be a heretic, the person has to belong to the religious body. Presbyterians and Unitarians held beliefs that some Friends considered heretical in the eighteenth and nineteenth centuries, yet Friends never accused them of heresy.

Debate on religious issues is not necessarily evidence of heresy. Disagreement only becomes heresy when it is in "...explicit opposition to ecclesiastial authority..."[2] Hannah Barnard's beliefs became dangerous when the Irish Friends divided. It was the potential for division that got David Sands and other Friends to challenge her beliefs. That those beliefs had been widely shared at an earlier time was less important than the threat they represented. Her unbelief combined with the political struggle within the body and produced the crisis. The threat she represented had to be eliminated, so Hannah Barnard was disowned.

At an earlier stage Hannah Barnard's views would have found agreement rather than challenge. The difference came because the elders had accepted ideas from the religious revival in other churches and made them their own. The elders had done this because they felt it was a return to the biblical focus of early Friends. Linking the new idea with their reinterpretation of early Friends beliefs allowed them to feel justified in imposing their reinterpretation on the Society of Friends. In Kurtz' terms, the elders redefined the form and substance of the trend to be critical of the acceptance of inspiration derived from the Inward Light. This drove the adherents of the Inward

146

Light together to form a movement to defend themselves against attack.[3]

Friends also fit two more parts of the pattern described by Kurtz.[4] First, doctrinal consequences came from redefining history and beliefs by both sides after division. And, second, Friends practice of disownment for uniting with other bodies or for non-attendance after a division was the ritual used to define and denounce heretics.

Disowning one person or a handful of people for heresy, however, is not the same as bringing on a large division. A division involves more people, and more points of disagreement. In a large division heresy is only one of the issues that divides the two groups. If it were the only one, a great deal of heat would be generated and a few, relative to the size of the body, would be removed from membership. However, in the process of exploring and debating the differences between them, people often find other issues on which to disagree. When the opposing stands coalesce to allow opposition parties to form, conditions become ripe for a division. Therefore, the time from the start of the debate on a heresy until the final break is longer than a disownment process. A break, however, is never inevitable as long as there are things — ideas, shared tradition, experience — that are more important than the divisive issues.

The causes of Friends divisions are far broader than the theological matters they have debated so strenuously. Friends form a part of the general society, and what affects society affects them just as deeply as other people. The social, ideological, political, racial, economic and other concerns that divide the body politic have also divided meetings. Any matter that is socially important can become a source of conflict for a meeting. If there are many important matters, they are all potentially divisive.

With several points of disagreement people will come to choose sides on all of them. For parties to form, contentious issues have to coalesce. That is, people have to form groups in which there is agreement on several of the issues. They then find themselves in opposition to other groups that have taken an opposing point of view on the same issues. However, if the issues do not coalesce, parties may not form. Then Friends will only have frequent noisy arguments. It takes time for matters to coalesce and for groups to form which disagree with each other on contentious issues.

Once opposing parties are formed, members of the opposing groups may begin to avoid each other. Avoidance over a long period of time destroys the coherence of the larger group and creates two separate groups which share the same identity.[5] Once this has happened, a seemingly trivial matter can lead to a division. Retrospectively, the issue may be given far greater importance than it deserves as the symbol of the break.

When a break is created at a yearly meeting gathering, it is usually a break in the groups who *represent* Friends at these gatherings. People at home in the local meeting are not immediately divided on the contentious issue. Therefore, after a break at yearly meeting, or quarterly meeting, representatives of the contending parties rush around trying to get support from the local Friends who were not present at the break. It is at this time that social linkages become important. Friends choose the sides that have most of their friends and relatives. When people are linked to both sides, they can be hurt quite badly by the conflict.

The representatives of each side do all they can to justify their views and the actions taken. They usually show their how their views either reflect "ancient principles" or certain important authorities in the Society. The efforts of Philadelphia Yearly Meeting (O) are illustrative. (See chapter 10 above.) The arguments used reiterate the rhetoric used earlier to remove heretics.

In a very interesting way, the efforts made to justify views and actions frequently re-define the orthodoxy of belief by selection from earlier forms. In this way a new orthodoxy is created which will be different from that of their opponents and, at the same time, unconsciously different from their own earlier forms. Further changes can then enter and, in time, a quite different form will be created.

In summary, the creation of a large division first requires the creation, definition and persecution of heresy. With that as a basis a division can come about when:

> a. Several socially important issues coalesce with the heresy; (the larger the number of issues, the bigger will be the size of the separating group);
> b. two groups of people who take opposite sides on the heresy and the issues;
> c. a period of time long enough to allow links between opposing groups to become less important than the links within the groups;
> d. the introduction of a new issue that also divides the groups; and,
> e. a concerted effort to justify and obtain support from Friends who were not present during the time of the break.

While this sets out the bare bones of the dynamic for a break,

Friends have divided quite often on the same matter. This matter has been both the focus and the symbol of their divisions. At the core is the problem of reconciling the inspiration received from the Inward Light with Holy Scripture. Early Friends saw little need to make this reconciliation. For them both came from the same source and hence were in perfect agreement. When people did something not in harmony with both they were regarded as having "run out from the Truth." However, even early Friends disagreed on what was meant by the "Truth." To discern the Truth required thought and understanding. It also required disciplined behavior. Only then could one be in the Light.

In the years after Fox died Friends built their internal organization, and codified their faith and expectations of behavior in the Discipline. The time of inward thinking allowed them to neglect Bible study in favor of inward worship. Neglect eventually produced a feeling that Bible study interfered with access to the Inward Light. When this became widespread, the evangelical revivals caused some Friends to rediscover the importance of the Bible. With rediscovery came the feeling that the gentle leadings of the Spirit might be fallible. These Friends could now treat the Inward Light as being less important.

By this time experience with the Inward Light had produced a series of beliefs that were in conflict with the new appreciation of the Bible. Old Testament accounts of war directed by God were redefined by this new appreciation as being infallible accounts. At the same time, Friends strong feelings about war had been reinforced in Ireland by their direct experience with the Irish troubles. It was at this point that the duality of Friends faith began to create serious problems. The assumption of harmony between Scripture and Inward Light could not now be made because the basic context had changed. Some Friends found greater strength in Scripture, while others trusted the Inward Light.

Both sides used early Friends and their ancient traditions to justify their views. Both sides understood a portion of the tradition, and both had departed from early Friends about an equal distance. In the process they created separate branches. Having parted ways, groups of Friends justified themselves by publishing selective readings of the old texts. This re-enforced their own views and moved them further away from the other branch creating two new and different contexts. The process was repeated as knowledge of the Bible changed with the development of biblical criticism and with new scientific discoveries. The consequence was to produce several branches of the Religious Society of Friends, each of which handled the duality of faith in its own way.

Today there is a surface assumption of difference made between Friends who practice "un-programmed" worship and those who have "programed" worship, that is, between people who sit in silence awaiting inspiration from the Inward Light and those who have planned their worship. However, there are important differences between groups who share the same form of worship. There are equally important similarities in faith between Friends who differ in their forms of worship. By using the duality of faith described, three groups of Friends can be distinguished. What follows below are simple caricatures rather than descriptions of the three groups. No Friend fits any of them, as faith is far from this simple. Also, the lines between the groups are not as stark as I have described them.

Group One: For this group the Bible is sometimes seen as a good book, sometimes as the best piece of religious literature. Some in this group feel a great proportion of the Bible is not relevant. Even those who would give credence to the Sermon on the Mount are quick to discount the Old Testament and the hard passages of Paul. Many would go to non-Christian spiritual sources as well. However, few at this extreme would limit themselves to the Bible for spiritual inspiration. Some might even refuse to read the Bible. If the inspiration given appears to disagree with the Scripture, then Scripture would be discounted. Being Quaker and following the Testimonies is more important than being Christian. When they look for God, they look inward in a contemplative way. Many would not grant personality to God at all, let alone gender, but see God as a creative force.

Friends who are at this end of the theological spectrum are more likely to be politically liberal. They will work for peace, social justice, and for the rights of minorities, including women and gays. Their religion focuses on the world and their social witness in it. These Friends feel comfortable with Eastern religious experience. They would make the Society of Friends into a Universal rather than a Christian Church.

Worship for Friends in this group is usually unprogrammed. It consists of waiting in silence for the inspiration of God. When inspiration is given, the message is shared and examined in the Light by everyone who hears it. These Friends feel that their form of worship is the original form, as practiced by Fox and other members of the early meetings. (What they forget is that waiting in silence at first was done only by members of the select meetings, by people who had been "baptized by the Spirit." In the early days most people attended the large and very vocal public gatherings. It was only after persecution stopped that silent meetings became the standard fare.) These Friends are likely to belong to yearly meetings that form part of Friends General Conference. Some Friends who are members of London Yearly Meeting would also feel more comfortable in this group.

Group Two: The great middle group of Friends feel that both the Inward Light and the Bible are important sources of religious inspiration. The two are interpreted and understood together in a way that allows for discussion and interpretation. Knowledge obtained from archeology, modern philosophy, science and other sources is used to add to the understanding. Scriptural accounts are reconciled with knowledge and inspiration. This reconciliation is taken seriously as the differences may be great. If it is not possible to bring the two sources of inspiration together, some Friends might lean one way, while others choose another way.

Worship for these Friends can be either unprogrammed and silent or programmed and pastoral. If it is programmed there is usually some provision for an unprogrammed time called "open worship" or "communion after the manner of Friends." Their worship can have hymns, prayers and sermons, all of which are planned prior to the start of worship. They also practice worship coming from silence, similar in concept to the first group of Friends. Many of this great middle group feel that both forms of worship are legitimate and complementary.

There is a creative tension in their religious life. Some members focus strongly on social witness, working for many of the same things for which the first group works. Their religious life is more likely to be church centered than centered on a social witness. They support both mission work and social work, and see the two as parts of the same. They may differ on degrees of emphasis, but the differences are reconciled. These Friends are likely to belong to yearly meetings that are a part of Friends United Meeting, belong jointly to Friends United Meeting and Friends General Conference, or to the various Conservative yearly meetings and London Yearly Meeting.

Group Three: The third group are Friends who are Bible literalists, and who regard the scriptural account as the inerrant and final authority. They can accept the Inward Light only if it is taken as evidence of the Holy Spirit and in no way disagrees with Scripture. Otherwise, the Inward Light may be suspect. Science and philosophy are potentially dangerous because they can lead people away from a belief in the Bible. Members use the Bible to answer life's daily issues as well as for their source of inspiration. They are not concerned with being called Quaker or with the historical testimonies as much as they are being Christians. Jesus and God are personal, with magnified

151

human traits, and can be known and spoken to.

Politically these Friends are conservative. They do not support the social causes, except for peace, that are so important to the first group. The basis for supporting any testimony — including peace — is how it relates to the Bible's imperatives. So their work for peace is in different arenas. They are made very uncomfortable by some of the radical statements of the first group. Their work is closely linked to their church life, which includes the missions they support. In many ways they are more at home with other denominations than they are with Friends at the opposite extreme. Friends who belong to yearly meetings forming part of the Evangelical Friends Alliance are usually members of this group.

B. Sacrilege

Sacrilege is behavior that is religiously outrageous. While an outrage can be committed by a non-believer, it only becomes a threat when it is done by a believer. Like heresy, it is defined by the extent of the threat it has for the religious system. One aspect of Friends Advices and Queries is to set out the form of behavior that is expected of Quakers. These have been revised from time to time but have always been treated with utmost respect. At one time they were read with regularity by most meetings. The custom was to answer the questions raised by them at quarterly meetings. The answers were then entered into the minutes and to form a State of Society report.

Friends Testimonies are embodied in the Advices and Queries. They set out how faith is to be acted out in life. Deviations from them are not violations of belief, they are errors of behavior that reflect on belief. What is at issue is the religious nature of the offense. The violations of Friends Testimonies that have been treated as sacrilege are the ones on credal statements, participation in the military, swearing of oaths, paying tithes and marrying without the approval of the meeting.

Marrying without the approval of the meeting has been both a very serious offense and not an offense at all. It was serious when Friends saw themselves as separate from the world; when they were trying to show that they were living a higher kind of life. The concern of the elders was to protect the integrity of their Society.

The large number of disownments began to decline when Friends perceived a threat to the size and growth of their meetings. When they recognized they had lost a significant number of young members, they stopped disowning people for marriage offenses. At this time they, in essence, redefined this form of behavior as not sacrilegious. Then, too, Friends have become less certain about all other forms of sacrilege. It has now reached the point where people are very unlikely to be disowned for any form of personal misbehavior before they have voluntarily chosen to stop participating. Even then they might be retained as nominal members.

C. To Conclude

There are some amusing ironies in the histories of Friends divisions that come from the very humanity of the people involved. One story was reported to me by the late Richard Newby, a prominent Indiana Friend and one-time clerk of Indiana Yearly Meeting, about the break that led to the creation of Nebraska Yearly Meeting. As the visiting speaker he was asked to select the closing hymn. The hymn he chose was no less than: "Blessed be the Tie That Binds." Even when Friends divide, there remain some ties that do bind. Blessed be those ties!

NOTES

Introduction

1. The version of the Journal used throughout this book is: Fox, George, *The Journal of George Fox*, revised edition by John L. Nickalls with an epilogue by Henry J. Cadbury and an introduction by Geoffrey F. Nuttall (Cambridge: University Press, 1952). Subsequently published (London: Religious Society of Friends ,1975).

2. Fox, pp. 602-4.

Chapter 1

1. Joan Thirsk, *The Agrarian History of England and Wales*, vol. IV 1500-1640 (Cambridge: University Press, 1967), pp. 17, 22-25 and 621.

2. Lewis Benson, *What did George Fox Teach about Christ* (Philadelphia: New Foundations Publication, 1976), pp. 14-15).

3. Hugh Barbour, *The Quakers in Puritan England*, (Richmond, Indiana: Friends United Press, 1985), p. 35 and 95.

4. Christopher Hill, *The World Turned Upside Down* (Harmondsworth, Middlesex, England: Penguin Books Ltd., 1975), pp. 93.

5. W.C. Braithwaite, T*he Beginnings of Quakerism* (Cambridge: University Press, 1955), p. 140. As quoted by Braithwaite, who writes that it may have come from William Dewsbury about 1653.

6. Hill, p. 14.

7. Hill, p. 72 and Alan Cole, "The Quakers and the English Revolution," *Past and Present*, No. 10 (Nov. 1956).

8. Henry Noel Brailsford, *The Levelers and the English Revolution* (Stanford, California: Stanford University Press, 1961), p. 396.

9. Hill, pp. 79 ff.

10. Hill, pp. 124-125

11. William Dewsbury, as quoted in Hugh Barbour and Arthur O. Roberts, *Early Quaker Writings* (Grand Rapids, Michigan: William B. Eerdmans, 1973), pp. 93-94. See also: W.W. Spurrier, "The Persecution of the Quakers in England: 1650-1714", *Ph. D. Thesis* (Chapel Hill: University of North Carolina, 1976), pp. 30 ff.

12. T. H. Hollingsworth, *Historical Demography* (Ithaca: Cornell University Press), pp. 79-87. The figures on Friends are even harder to come by. Usually there are estimates, many of which are highly suspect. Braithwaite's estimates for 1660 were 30 to 40,000 and for 1670 were about 10,000 more. Rowntree suggests 55 to 60,000 in 1680; see: Spurrier, pp. 199 ff (See chapter two, note #3 for ref.).

13. For a good discussion on the differences between Ranters and Quakers see: McGregor, J.F. "Ranterism and the Development of Early Quakerism", *Journal of Religious History*, Vol. 9, 1976-7, pp. 349-363.

14. Hugh Barbour and Arthur O. Roberts, *Early Quaker Writings* (Grand Rapids, Michigan: William B. Eerdmans, 1973), pp. 28-31 and 567-576.

15. Braithwaite, pp. 135-136.

16. As quoted in Braithwaite, p. 136. Later this was used to justify the creation of a pastoral system among Friends in the United States.

17. Braithwaite, pp. 142-143, as quoted from Fox "...Concerning our monthly and quarterly meetings..." who wrote it in 1689.

18. Braithwaite, pp. 147, ff.

19. William McMurray, "Notes on the History of the Bull and Mouth Meeting House, London, 1352-1887" (extracted from "A City Church Chronicle" and quoted — with no page or date reference given), *Journal of the Friends Historical Society*, vol. 12 (1915), pp. 30-31.

20. William George Bittle, "James Nayler: A Study in Seventeenth Century Quakerism," *Ph. D. Thesis* (Kent State University, 1975), p. 155.

21. Bittle, Ch. 1 and pp. 130-131; and Fox, pp. 63, 178, and 337-338.

22. Fox, pp. 182-189 and Kenneth L. Carrol, "Martha Simmonds, A Quaker Enigma", *Journal of the Friends Historical Society*, vol. 53, (1972), no. 1, pp. 31-52.

23. Bittle, pp. 205-214; Carrol, pp. 43-44; and, Emilia Fogelklou Norlind, "The Atonement of George Fox", *Pendle Hill Pamphlet #166*, pp. 12-14.

24. Bittle, pp. 221-224; Carrol, pp. 44-45; and Fogelklou.

25. Bittle, pp. 234, as quoted.

26. Bittle, pp. 276-298.

27. Geoffrey Nuttall, *Studies in Christian Enthusiasm* (Wallingford, Pa.: Pendle Hill, 1948), p. 71.

Chapter 2

1. Braithwaite, p. 320.

2. Fox, 399.

3. For perhaps the best summary of the persecution of Friends see: Spurrier, W.W. "The Persecution of the Quakers in England: 1650-1714", *Ph. D. Thesis*, (Chapel Hill: University of North Carolina, 1976). This thesis summarizes and extends the account in Joseph Besse, *A Collection of Sufferings of the Quakers* (London, 1753, 2 vols.).

4. Fox, p. 398.

5. Thomas Ellwood, "The History of the Life of Thomas Ellwood: Written by Himself" in Evans, W. And T. Evans (Eds.), *The Friends Library; Comprising Journals Doctrinal Treatises, and Other Writings of the Religious Society of Friends*, vol. 7, p. 243.

6. Fox, pp. 285, 288, 292, 308-309, 312, and 314.

7. Fox, p. 528.

8. Fox, *Works*, vol. 8, pp. 132.

9. Kenneth L. Carrol, *John Perrot: Early Quaker Schismatic* (London: Friends Historical Society, 1971), pp. 11-33.

10. Rufus M. Jones, *The Quakers in the American Colonies* (London: MacMillan and Co., 1911), p. 276. See also: James Bowden, History of the Society of Friends in America (London, Charles Gilpin, 1850), vol. I, pp. 350 ff.

11. As quoted in Barbour and Roberts, pp. 254-255, from the *History of the*
156

Life of Thomas Elwood).

12. Quoted by Barbour and Roberts from Robert Rich, *Hidden Thoughts brought to Light, or the Discord of the Grand Quakers Among Themselves,* (London, 1678), p. 7.

13. Apparently Richard Farnsworth had recognized this as early as the summer of 1663. See W. C. Braithwaite, *The Second Period of Quakerism,* 2nd. Ed. (Cambridge: University Press, 1961), p. 243 and Elbert Russell, *The History of Quakerism* (New York: The MacMillan Company, 1942), p. 128.

14. Fox, p. 411. George Fox, "The Spirit of Envy, Lying, and Persecution, made Manifest", London, 1663. Braithwaite, *Beginnings,* p. 275 and Carrol, pp. vii, 61,66 and 83 ff.

15. Braithwaite, *Second Period,* p. 240 and Carrol, pp. 64, 77 and 82.

16. Elfrida Vipont, *George Fox and the Valiant Sixty* (London: Hamish Hamilton, 1975), p. 129.

17. H. R. Smith, "The Wilkinson-Story Controversy in Reading", *Journal of the Friends Historical Society,* vol. I (1903-1904), pp. 57-61; and Braithwaite, *Second Period,* p. 294.

18. Elizabeth Stirredge gives a vivid account of her problems in dealing with the issue in: "The Life and Christian Testimony of that Faithful Servant of the Lord, Elizabeth Stirredge, who departed this life, at her house at Hemstead, in Hertfordshire, in the Seventy-second Year of Age. Written by her own Hand [1711]." In Evans and Evans (Eds.), vol. II, 1838, pp. 194 ff.

19. See: Fox, p. 668

20. Vipont, *George Fox and the Valiant Sixty,* pp. 128-129.

21. Braithwaite, *Second Period,* p. 292; William Sewell, *The History of the Rise, Increase and Progress of the Christian People Called Quakers; Intermixed with Several Remarkable Occurrences* (London: William Phillips, 1811), p. 561; and Allen C. Thomas, and Richard H. Thomas, *A History of the Society of Friends in America* (Philadelphia: John C. Winston & Co. 1895), p. 199. [Note: the pagination is unusual because it was retained from the time when the work first appeared as a portion of vol. XII in the American Church History Series].

22. Robert Barclay, "Anarchy of the Ranters and Other Libertines".

23. Braithwaite, pp. 299-300.

24. Howard R. Smith, "The Wilkinson-Story Controversy in Reading", *Journal of the Friends Historical Society*, Vol. I, 1903-4, pp. 57-61.

25. Fox, p. 104.

26. Hugh Barbour, *The Quakers in Puritan England*, p. 223.

Chapter 3

1. As quoted by John E. Pomfret, *The Province of West New Jersey, 1609-1702; A History of the Origin of and American Colony* (Princeton, N.J.: Princeton University Press, 1956), p. 93.

2. Garry B. Nash, *Quakers and Politics: Pennsylvania, 1681-1726*, (Princeton: Princeton University Press, 1968) ch. I.

3. Nash, pp. 49 ff.

4. Rufus Jones has difficulty accepting Keith's influence on Barclay. Both W.C. Braithwaite and D. Elton Trueblood claim Keith did affect Barclay. In a personal note Barbour finds the doubts about the effect of Keith on Barclay to be not very serious when an examination is made of their time together in Aberdeen and their early books.

5. Ethyn Williams Kirby, *George Keith, 1658-1716* (New York and London: Appleton-Century Company Incorporated, 1942), pp. 42-45 and Pomfret, pp. 243-244.

6. Kirby, pp. 55-57.

7. See Crook in Barbour and Roberts, pp. 544 ff. and the London Yearly Meeting epistle of 1691.

8. As quoted in Robert Proud, *The History of Pennsylvania in That Province Under the First Proprietor and Governor William Penn, in 1681, till After the Year 1742*, (Philadelphia: Printed and Sold by Zachariah Poulson, Junior, 1797), vol. I., p. 364.

9. As quoted in Proud, pp. 365-368 and by Bowden, vol. II., pp. 86-90.

10. Kirby, pp. 70 ff. and Jones, R., pp. 447 ff.

11. The number who were disowned or withdrew is not clear. However, estimates of 500 were made, see Kirby, p. 77 and Frederick B. Tolles, *Meeting House and Counting House: The Quaker Merchants of Colonial Philadelphia* (Chapel Hill: University of North Carolina Press, 1948), p. 34.

12. See Kirby, pp. 80-85 for a more complete account of the proceedings.

13. Proud, vol. I, p. 365.

14. Thomas, pp. 232-233.

15. John Gough, *A History of the People Called Quakers; From Their First Rise to the Present Time. Compiled from Authentic Records and from the Writings of that People* (in four volumes) (Dublin: Printed for Robert Jackson, 1789), vol. III, p. 323.

16. Proud, vol. I.

17. J. William Frost, J. William, *The Keithian Controversy in Early Pennsylvania* (Norwood, Pa., Norwood Editions: 1980). From Frost's point of view there would have been not division without Keith. And, what is most interesting, he feels that the major issue was religious, particularly the parts as contained in Keith's confession of faith. See the Introduction.

18. Jon Butler, "Gospel Order Improved; The Keithian Schism and the Exercise of Quaker Ministerial Authority in Pennsylvania," *William and Mary Quarterly*, vol. 31, No. 3, July, 1974, p. 452. Butler feels that although the early troubles were concerned with doctrinal issues, the final break came over the challenge to ministerial authority.

19. Pomfret, pp. 246 ff.

20. Melvin B. Endy, William Penn and Early Quakerism (Princeton, N.J., Princeton University Press: 1973), pp. 77.

21. Endy, p. 236

22. For an account of the decline of the people who had withdrawn with Keith, see: Butler, Jon, "Into Pennsylvania's Spiritual Abyss: the Rise and Fall of the Later Keithians, 1693-1703," *The Pennsylvania Magazine of History and Biography*, April 1977, p. 151-170.

23. Butler, p. 452.

Chapter 4

1. Arthur Raistrick, *Quakers in Science and Industry: Being an Account of the Quaker contributions to Science and Industry During the 17th. and 18th. Centuries* (New York: Augustine M. Kelley, Publishers, 1968), pp. 48-50.

2. Raistrick, p. 231

3. Hugh Doncaster, *Organization and Business Meetings* (London: Friends Home Service Committee, 1958). He covers their activities very nicely and what he describes for London Yearly Meeting was paralleled by other yearly meetings.

4. Howard H. Brinton, *Friends for Three Hundred Years* (London: George Allen and Unwin, 1953, p. 126-7.

5. Lloyd, Arnold, *Quaker Social History, 1669-1738* (London: Longmans, Green and Co., 1950) pp. 42-44.

6. See Raistrick, who describes their accomplishments.

7. As quoted by Raistrick, p. 231.

8. Tolles, F., p. 49.

9. Richard Bauman, *For the Reputation of Truth; Politics, Religion and Conflict Among the Pennsylvania Quakers, 1750-1800* (Baltimore and London: The Johns Hopkins Press, 1971), pp. 2-4.

10. See: Jack D. Marietta, "The Growth of Quaker Self-Consciousness in Pennsylvania, 1720-1748," In J. William Frost and John M. Moore, [eds], *Seeking the Light,* Wallingford and Haverford, Pennsylvania; Pendle Hill Publications & Friends Historical Association, 1986.

11. J. William Frost, *The Quaker Family in Colonial America* (New York: St. Martin's Press, 1973), pp. 100 and 159.

12. Elbert Russell, *The History of Quakerism* (New York: The MacMillan Company, 1942), p. 204.

13. Bauman, pp. 5-7.

14. See: Bauman, who provides the details of these events.

15. Bauman, pp. 65-110, provides a fairly complete account of the incident

and of the "Friendly Association for Regaining and Preserving Peace with Indians by Pacific Measures."

16. Bernard Bailyn, *The Ideological Origins of the American Revolution* (Cambridge, Mass.: The Belknap Pres of Harvard University Press, 1967).

17. Frost, p. 205 and Nash, pp. 544-584.

18. Frost, pp. 159-160.

19. Jack D. Marietta, *The Reformation of American Quakerism*, 1748-1783 (Philadelphia: University of Pennsylvania Press, 1984), pp. 257-73. This is a summary of Marietta's views of the changes that came as a result of the revolution. His bias shows through unconsciously when he refers to Friends lack of identification with "American" society, clearly using the word in its modern patriotic context.

20. By the end of the war Bauman, p. 165, reports 908 disownments for participating in revolutionary activities.

21. For a description of the move north and the formation of new meetings in Canada see Arthur Dorland, *A History of the Society of Friends* (Quakers) *in Canada* (Toronto: The Ryerson Press, 1968).

22. Marietta, p. 273.

23. G. M. Trevelyan, *Illustrating English Social History*, Vol. III (London: Longmans, Green and Co., 1942), p. 100.

24. Among historians there is no general agreement as to which of them was meaningful and which was not. Jones, for example, writes that the testimony against hat honor, the removal of a hat by a person to someone else of higher social standing, "... possessed little real spiritual value... (*Later Periods of Quakerism*, Vol. I, p. 169)". W. C. Braithwaite, however, disagrees with him, see *The Beginnings of Quakerism*, pp. 47, and 49ff.

25. Rufus Jones, *Quakers in the American Colonies*, p. 524; Marietta, pp. 6-7; and, Bauman, p. 165.

26. Frost, p. 97; and, Marietta, pp. 6 and 16.

27. See: "The Disownment of John Bartram", *Bulletin of Friend's Historical Association*, Vol. 17, No. 1 (Spring, 1928), pp. 16-22. Henry J. Cadbury was then editor of the *Bulletin* and felt the minute was important enough to be quoted in full.

28. Russell, p. 107.

29. Russell, p. 222.

30. Russell, pp. 178-9, 229-31. For a more complete description of Quaker Quietism, see Ch. 18.

31. This derived from William Penn's ideal that people should be allowed freedom of conscience. See: Bauman, p.1.

Chapter 5

1. See: Elbert Russell, *The History of Quakerism*; Rufus Jones, *Later Periods of Quakerism*, Vol. I; Bliss Forb*ush*, *Elias Hicks; Quaker Liberal* (New York: Columbia University Press, 1956); Robert W. Doherty, *The Hicksite Separation: A Sociological Analysis of Religious Schism in Early Nineteenth Century America* (New Brunswick, N.J.: Rutgers University Press, 1967); Seebohm, B. (Ed.) *Memoirs of the Life and Labours of Stephen Grellet* (London: A.W. Bennett, 1860); and others.

2. Thomas Evans makes much of this in his apology in support of the stand taken by Orthodox Friends after the division in Philadelphia in 1827.

3. Henry J. Cadbury, "The Disownment of John Bartram", *Bulletin of the Friends Historical Association*, Vol. 17, No. 1, 1928, pp. 16-22.

4. Marietta, p. 6. His percentages lead to questions about the irregular numbers they produce; therefore, the percentage give is probably in error.

5. Lester R. Kurtz, "The Politics of Heresy", *American Journal of Sociology*, Vol. 66, no. 6 (May, 1983), p. 1087.

6. Kurtz, p. 1088.

7. Kurtz, p. 1089-90.

8. See: Allen C. Thomas and Richard H. Thomas, pp. 249 ff.

9. See: *Isabel Grubb, Quakers in Ireland, 1654-1900* (London: Swarthmore Press, Ltd., 1927), pp. 121-122, and Rufus Jones. Sands was described by Rufus Jones as "... the foremost representative of evangelical views..." See: vol., p. 301.

10. William Hodgson, *Society of Friends in the Nineteenth Century; A Historical View of the Successive Convulsions and Schisms Therin During that Period* (Philadelphia: Smith, English and Co., 1875), pp. 29-35. See also Jones, Vol. I., pp. 236-298.

11. Jones, Vol., I p. 301

12. Jones, Vol. I, p. 299.

13. Hodgson, p. 39.

14. Jones, Vol. I, p. 300.

15. Forbush, p. 118.

16. See Hodgson, pp. 44-50 for a rather ones sided view of the affair and Jones, Vol. I, pp.299-306 for a less biased account.

17. H. Larry Ingle, *Quakers in Conflict: The Hicksite Reformation* (Knoxville: The University of Tennessee Press, 1986), p. 10.

18. Ingle, p. 12, who footnotes Forbush, p. 195.

19. Hodgson, pp. 51-99.

20. See: Forbush, pp. 170-173.

21. See: Forbush, pp. 188-189; Doherty, p. 29; and Jones, Vol. I., p. 460.

22. Ingle, p. 18

23. Ingle, pp. 103-5.

24. As quoted by Jones, Vol. I, pp. 461.

25. See: Russell, p. 298 and Jones, Vol. I, pp. 460-464.
    Jones writes: "the statement was adopted by the Meeting for Sufferings and an edition was printed for circulation.
    "When the minutes of the Meeting for Sufferings were read for approval in the Yearly Meeting in 1823, a great storm was raised, for it was at once recognized that when these minutes were approved, this statement of doctrine would stand as the official position of the Yearly Meeting. (p. 463)"

26. Ingle, pp. 84-86 summarizes the meeting that caused both Jonathan Evans and Elias Hicks irreparable harm.

27. Forbush, p. 20.

28. Ingle pp. 103-105.

29. Ingle pp. 181-188

30. John Comly is outstanding here, see Thomas, pp. 258-259 and Jones, Vol. I, p. 465.

31. Ingle, p. 122

32. Ingle, p. 154

33. Ingle, pp. 157-158.

34. For a more complete description of these events see Ingle pp. 160-180.

35. See: Ingle, ch. 10.

36. Jones, p. 468.

37. Jeremiah J. Foster, *An Authentic Report of the Testimony in cause at issue in the Court of Chancery of the State of New Jersey between Thomas L. Shotwell, complainant and Joseph Hendrickson and Stacy Decow, defendants* (Philadelphia: J. Harding, 1831), vol. II, pp. 455-456.

38. Doherty, p. 64.

39. See: Ingle, ch. 11 for many of the details of these events.

40. Doherty, p. 42-69.

41. Hodgson, p. 130.

42. Hodgson, p. 105.

43. Jones, vol. I, p. 435.

44. Foster, p. xvi.

45. Ingle, p. 223-224.

46. Doherty, p. 23.

47. Doherty, p. 79.

Chapter 6

1. J. Foster, as quoted by Seebohm, B., *Memoirs of the Life and Gospel Labours of Stephen Grellet*, vol. II, p. 39.

2. See: Forbush, p. xiv.

3. Thomas Shillitoe, *Journal of the Life, Labours, and Travels of Thomas Shillitoe, in the Service of the Gospel of Jesus Christ* (London: Harvey and Darton, 1839), vol. II, pp. 311-312.

4. New York Yearly Meeting Minutes of 5th month 27th, 1828.

5. T. Evans, "Census of Friends and Hicksites from records to Meeting for Sufferings. 1835"

6. W. Hobbs, "Some Few Speeches of the difficulties among Friends at Blue River Occasioned by the Doctrines of Elias Hicks as taken down by William Hobbs." As Quoted by Barbara Chase in "The Hicksite Separation in Indiana Yearly Meeting," and unpublished typsecript dated March 11, 1977, p. 8.

7. Ohio Yearly Meeting (H) Minutes, 1828, pp. 12-13.

8. Indiana Yearly Meeting (H) Minutes, 1828, opening paragraph.

9. See: Ingle, p. 230.

10. See: Russell, pp. 317-318; Thomas, pp. 262-263; Jones, *Later Periods*, vol. I, pp. 474-488; Forbush, pp. 249ff; and K. Morse, *A History of Conservative Friends; Consisting of a History of Ohio Yearly Meeting, Somerset Monthly Meeting (Ohio) and other Conservative bodies in America* (Barnesville, Ohio: Kenneth S.P. Morse, 1962), p. 4 ff.

11. Shillitoe, vol. II, pp. 343-4. Also see Ingle, p. 241.

12. See: Edwin B. Bronner, *"The Other Branch": London Yearly Meeting and*

the Hicksites, 1827-1912, (London: Friends Historical Society, 1975).

13. Robert N. Bellah, "Religious Evolution", In Roland Robertson [ed]. *Sociology of Religion* (Harmondsworth, Middlesex, England: Penguin Books, 1969), p. 289.

14. Ohio Yearly Meeting (H) Minutes, 1828, p. 1

15. Forbush, p. 248.

16. See: Dorland, Arthur G., *The Quakers in Canada, A History* (Toronto: The Ryerson Press, 1968), pp. 157-179.

Chapter 7

1. David J. Hall, "Membership Statistics of the Society of Friends, 1800-1850", *Journal of the Friends Historical Association*, vol. 52 (1968), No. 1, pp. 96-100; and, Elizabeth Isichei, *Victorian Quakers* (London: Oxford University Press, 1970), p. 44.

2. Isaac Crewdson, *A Beacon to the Society of Friends* (London: Hamilton and Co., 1836), p. 6.

3. Jones, *Later Periods*, vol. I, pp. 489-507 and Isichei, pp. 44-47.

4. Anna Braithwaite Thomas (Ed.), *J. Bevan Braithwaite; A Friend of the Nineteenth Century* (Philadelphia: The Book Committee of Philadelphia Yearly Meeting of Friends, 1916), pp. 64-65.

5. Isichei, pp. 48-52.

6. *Epistles from Yearly Meeting of Friends held in London*, Vol. 2, p. 272. See also the London *Discipline*, 1906, vol. I, pp. 13-14.

Chapter 8

1. F.B. Tolles, *Meeting House and Counting House*, (Chapel Hill: University of North Carolina Press, 1948), p. vii. He was paraphrasing Rufus Jones' King's Chapel Lecture on the religious history of New England.

2. Ohio Yearly Meeting (Hicksite) *Minutes* of the 4th. to 12th. of 9th. month, 1828. p. 3.

3. William Hodgson, *The Society of Friends in the Nineteenth Century: A Historical View of the Successive Convulsions and Schisms therein During that Period*, 2 vols. (Philadelphia: Smith, English and Co., 1875), vol. 2, p. 31.

4. Robert William Fogel, and Stanley L. Engerman, *Time on Cross; The Economics of American Negro Slavery* (Boston and Toronto: Little, Brown and Company, 1974).

5. Indiana Yearly Meeting (Orthodox), *Minutes* 1839, p. 6.

6. Indiana yearly Meeting (O), *Minutes*, 1839, p. 21.

7. Jones, *Quakers in the American Colonies*, pp. 588 ff.

8. The letter was dated 21st to 31st of Fifth month, 1845 published in Indiana Yearly Meeting Minutes, 1846 p. 2.

9. The British Friend, 4th. Month 20th., 1843, p. 60.

10. Thomas E. Drake, *Quakers and Slavery in America* (New Haven: Yale University Press, 1950), p. 167.

11. James Harris Norton, "Quakers West of the Alleghenies and in Ohio to 1861" Ph.D. Thesis (Case Western Reserve University, 1965), pp. 212-218.

12. Yearly Meeting of Friends who have adopted the Congregational Order of Church Government, minutes of the 26th of 10th month, 1850. See also Willard Heiss, "Chronicles of John and Zachariah; and Incident in the History of Midwestern Friends", *Bulletin of the Friends Historical Association*, Vol. 46, No. 2, 1957, pp. 99-105.

13. Thomas, pp. 21-31.

Chapter 9

1. F. B. Tolles, "The New-Light Quakers of Lynn and New Bedford", *The New England Quarterly*, vol. 32, no. 3, pp. 291-319, see especially p. 317. Also see G.A. Rawlyk, *Ravished by the Spirit; Religious Revivals, Baptists, and Henry Alline* (Kingston and Montreal: McGill-Queen's Press, 1984), for a description of the movement at an early period in the Canadian Maritimes.

2. Tolles, pp. 297-301.

3. Tolles, pp. 308 and 314.

4. Tolles, pp. 303 ff.

5. See: Rufus Jones, *Later Periods*, vol. I, pp. 511 ff.

6. Jones, vol. I, p. 520; Morse, p. 6; and, W.C. Braithwaite, vol. 2, pp. 220-221)

7. Jones, vol. I, p. 521

8. Hodgson, vol. II, p. 49.

9. Jones, vol. I, pp. 511-527; Thomas, pp. 266-269; Russell, pp. 349-353; and, Hodgson, vol. II, pp. 49-111.

10. Thomas, p. 267.

Chapter 10

1. J. Bevan Braithwaite, *Memoirs of Joseph John Gurney; With Selections from his Journal and Correspondence.* In Two Volumes (Norwich: Fletcher and Alexander, 1854), vol. I, p. 538.

2. For a report on this see *The Friend* (Philadelphia). Vol. XXVIII, Ninth Month 16th., 1854., p. 7.

3. Balthasar Henry Meyer, & Caroline E. MacGill [Eds.], *History of Transportation in the United States Before 1860* (Washington: The Carnegie Institute of Washington, 1917), p. 501. In some ways this is a curious book. The material is excellent and is beautifully written and presented. The curiosity is in the assigned authorship. It is written by the second person listed in the bibliographic index, and on the title page. The first person listed wrote the foreword and was the director of the Institute.

4. W.B. Taber, Jr., "The Expanding World of Ohio kin the latter part of the Nineteenth Century", *Quaker History*, vol. 56, No. 1, pp. 18-33.

5. Taber, p. 21.

6. James L. Burke, and Donald E. Bensch, *Mount Pleasant and the Early Quakers of Ohio* (Columbus, Ohio: The Ohio Historical Society, 1975), p. 18.

7. Howard Brinton, "Friends for 75 Years," *Bulletin of the Friends Historical*

Association, Vol. 49, No. 1, p. 7.

8. See for example: *The Friend* (Philadelphia), Vol. XXVIII, p. 327 and p. 351.

9. *The Friend,* p. 327.

10. Brinton, pp. 7-8.

11. Brinton, p. 7

12. Minutes of Baltimore Yearly Meeting (of Primitive Friends), 23.10,1854, p. 2.

13. Baltimore Y. M. p. 1

14. Baltimore Y.M. p. 2

15. Baltimore Y.M. See, for example, the minutes of 20-22. 10. 1862, p. 95.

Chapter 11

1. There is some evidence that Friends were not all behaving in a manner that had been expected of them at an earlier age, see for example: Anon, *Quakerism: or the Story of My Life. By a Lady who for Forty Years was a Member of the Society of Friends.* (Philadelphia: J.W. Moore, 1852). She described how Friends found a way of retaining their respectability within the Society by not paying tithes. At the same time they stayed out of prison because the state gave them credit for having paid their tithes. The mechanism was simple: When they were found guilty of not having paid their tithes, some of their goods, normally the household's sterling silver, were seized. The goods were then sold publicly to cover the size of the fine and were usually bought by a silversmith. The silver was cleaned and repaired and then the Friends from whom they were originally seized were offered the opportunity of buying it back. The price paid covered the cost of the fine and the silversmith's work. As the same smiths bought the silver each time it was sold publicly, and they knew the Friends from whom it was seized, they could feel sure of a profit. In return the Friends got their silver cleaned and repaired. These Friends were also credited with having paid their fine and tithe by proxy without running afoul of the Discipline.

The lady who wrote the book was eventually disowned for her critical views of the elders who behaved in this fashion. She was quite disillusioned by Friends as she wrote:

To consider the Society of Friends as a religious body, is a monstrous stretch of the imagination. Respectable, active, intelligent, benevolent, useful, wealthy and influential, they undoubtedly are; but a man may be all this, and yet devoid of that religion, without which he can never hope for life eternal... (p. x)

2. Isichei, pp. 53-54.

3. Isichei, pp. 55-56.

4. See: Fred Haslam, *A Record of Experience with and on Behalf of The Religious Society of Friends in Canada: and with the Canadian Ecumenical Movement, 1921-1967 with some thoughts for the Future* (Toronto: privately printed, 1968).

5. Canadian Yearly Meeting Minute #61 1969.

6. See: *The Friend* (London), vol. 125, no. 47, p. 1455 for a letter containing their final epistle and no. 49, p. 1520 for a report from the Meeting for Sufferings.

7. R. C. Scott, "Authority or Experience; John Wilhelm Rowntree and the Dilemma of 19th. Century British Quakerism," *Journal of the Friends Historical Society*, vol. 49, no. 2 (Spring, 1960), p. 75.

8. *Essays and Reviews*, 2nd. Ed., 1860.

9. A.B. Thomas, pp. 230-6.

10. A.B. Thomas, p. 227.

11. Scott, pp. 77-78.

12. Isichei, p. 62. See also, J.B. Braithwaite *Journal*, of 20th. 4th month, 1871.

13. Isichei, pp. 63-65 and Scott, p. 80.

Chapter 12

1. For an account of the development of evangelicalism and revivalism see: Timothy L. Smith, *Revivalism* and *Social Reform in Mid-Nineteenth-Century America* (New York: Abingdon press, 1957). he distinguishes between what he referred to as "Evangelical Arminiamism" and "Evangelical Calvinism". The difference between the two seems to him to be "... more a matter of custom than of creed... (p. 33)

2. T.L. Smith, pp. 45 and 62.

3. Melvin E. Dieter, *The Holiness Revival of the Nineteenth Century; Studies in Evangelicalism, No. 1* (Metuchen, N.J. & London: The Scarecrow Press, 1980), p. 159.

4. Dieter, p. 191

5. Elbert Russell, *The History of Quakerism* (New York: The MacMillan Company, 1942). He refers to this on p. 281. See also: Allan C. Thomas, and Richard H. Thomas, *A History of Friends in America* (Philadelphia: John C. Weston, 1895), on p. 121. See: "The Friend" (Philadelphia), vol. II, pp. 413ff.; and, vol. v., pp. 268-270.

6. T. L. Smith, p. 62 and 72.

7. T.L. Smith, T.L., p. 80.

8. T.L. Smith, T.L., p. 82 and 152. He footnotes Elisha Bates *Doctrines of Friends* that he called "... The platform of the evangelical party of the Quakers..." Also , see Dieter, p. 191.

9. Richard E. Wood, "Interacting with a Society in Conflict: Evangelical Quaker Acculturation in the Upper Mississippi Valley, 1850-1875." Presented at the gathering of the Friends Historians and Archivists at Malone College, June 1986.

10.Thomas D. Hamm, *The Transformation of American Quakerism: Orthodox Friends, 1800-1907,* (Bloomington, Ind.: Indiana University Press, 1988).

11. See: Lawrence E. Barker, "The Development of the Pastoral Pattern in Indiana yearly Meeting of the Religious Society of Friends," *M.A. Thesis,* Earlham School of Religion, 1963., p. 32. He quotes from *Charles A. Coffin, A Quaker Pioneer,* compiled by Mary Coffin Johnson and Percival Coffin (Richmond: Nicholson, 1923), p. 115. Also see: John William Buys, "Quakers in Indiana in the Nineteenth Century", *Ph.D. Thesis* (University of Florida, 1973), pp. 277-278.

12. Indiana yearly Meeting Minutes, 1880, p. 21 and 1881, p. 40. Also mentioned in: Buys, p. 36; and by Barker, pp. 40-44.

13. Buys, p. 281

14. Barker, p. 44.

15. This argument is essentially the one used by such people as Charles M. Woodman, *Quakers Find a Way; Their Discoveries in Practical Thinking,* (Indianapolis: Bobbs-Merrill, 1950), p. 150 and Walter R. Williams, *The Rich Heritage of Quakerism* (Grand Rapids, Michigan: Eerdmans, 1962), p. 200.

16. Howard Brinton, in *Friends for 300 Years*, (London: George Allen and Unwin, 1953).

17. Barker, p. 58.

18. David E.W. Holden, "Membership Numbers and the 1902-1904 North Carolina Yearly Meeting Division", *The Southern Friend,* Vol. VI, Spring, 1984, No. 1, pp. 36-39.

19. Barker, p. 57

20. Buys, p. 160. He refers to the Report of the Indiana Yearly Meeting Executive Committee for Relief of Colored Freedmen, 1864, p. 21).

21. David C. LeShana, *Quakers in California; the Effects of 19th. Century Revivalism on Western Quakerism* (Newberg, Oregon The Barclay Press, 1969, p. 166). LeShana footnotes Edward Grubb *Separations, Their Causes and Effects*, p. 109 to suggest that the first person to be named a Quaker Pastor was Luke Woodward and quoting from Alexander H. Hay's M.A. Thesis "The Rise of the Pastoral System in the Society of Friends 1850-1900," that the earliest possible date was 1872.

22. Buys, p. 285. Also see: Indiana Yearly Meeting Minutes, 1896, pp. 16-17.

23. Walker, Howard Earl, "The Conception of a Ministry in the Quaker Movement and a Survey of its development", *Ph. D. Thesis,* (University of Edinburgh, 1952), p. 214.

24. Buys, pp. 286-287. Donald G. Good, "Elisha Bates American Quaker Evangelical in the Early Nineteenth Century", *Ph.D. Thesis* (University of Iowa, 1967), pp. 340-347 and *passim.* Elisha Bates, *The Doctrines of Friends; or, Principles of the Christian Religion, as Held by the Society of Friends Commonly Called Quakers* (Mount Pleasant Printed and Published by the Author, 1824), p. 224.

25. Errol T. Elliott, *Quakers on the American Frontier; A History of The Westward Migrations, Settlements, and Development of Friends on the American Continent* (Richmond, Indiana: Friends United press, 1969), p. 269. Also see: Buys, p. 288 and Good.

26. From a letter of Joel Bean to Rufus Jones as quoted by Brinton, Howard H., "the Revival Movement in Iowa: a Letter from Joel Bean to Rufus M. Jones," *Bulletin of the Friends Historical Association*, vol. 50, no. 1, 1961, pp. 105.

27. Buys, p. 288, and Elliott, p. 269, whom he cites.

28. See: *Indiana Yearly Meeting Minutes*, 1886, p. 69 and Buys, p. 292.

29. Allen Jay; Mahalah Jay; and, Thomas N. White, eds. *Proceedings including Declaration of Christian Doctrine, of the General Conference of Friends, held in Richmond, Ind., U.S.A., 1887* (Richmond, Indiana: Nicholson & Bro., 1887), pp. 6-8.

30. Both Earl Redding, "A Report to the General Board of Friends United Meeting Concerning the History of the Affirmation of Faith and Uniform Discipline of the Five Years Meeting of Friends," (Oskaloosa, Iowa: mimeograph), June, 1974, p. 1 and Buys, p. 294, agree on this matter..

31. J. Bevan Braithwaite was named to the committee along with William Nicholson, George Grubb, James Cary Thomas, James Wood, Joseph Moore, Barnabas C. Hobbs, Mary W. Tomas, Benjamin Trueblood, George Gilett, Jacob Baker, and Mahalah Jay, see: Redding, p. 7.

32. *Proceedings of the Conference of Friends*, 1887, p. 18.

33. *Proceedings of the Conference of Friends*, 1887, pp. 65-66, 173-177, and 310. Redding, pp. 13-20.

34. As quoted by Mark Minear, *Richmond 1887; A Quaker Drama Unfolds* (Richmond, Indiana; Friends United press, 1987) , p. 132, from *Proceedings of the General Conference of Friends*, p. 307.

35. Quoted by Minear, pp. 132-133, from Jay, *Proceedings of Friends Conference*, 1888, pp. 281-82.

36. J. Brent Bill, *David B. Updegraff; Quaker Holiness Preacher* (Richmond Indiana: Friends United Press, 1983), pp. 15-17.

37. Bill, p. 17

38. See: Bill, pp. 25-34, where he quotes from David B. Updegraff, *An Address to Ohio Yearly Meeting on the Ordinances and Position of Friends Generally in Relation to Them* (Columbus: William g. Hubbard & Co., Publishers, 1885).

39. See: Bill, pp. 15-42 for insight in David Updegraff's beliefs.

Chapter 13

1. Elliott, p. 108-110.

2. Elliott, p. 109-110.

3. Elliott, p. 125.

4. Wilmer Tjossem, *Quaker Sloopers: From the Fjords to the Prairies* (Richmond, Indiana: Friends United Press, 1984), pp. 10-11.

5. Tjossem, p. 23-29.

6. Elliott, pp. 116-117.

7. From a Letter of Joel Bean to Rufus Jones as quoted by Brinton, Howard H., "The Revival Movement in Iowa; A Letter from Joel Bean to Rufus M. Jones," in *Bulletin of the Friends Historical Association*, vol. 50, No. 1, Spring Number, 1961, p. 105.

8. Lewis T. Jones, *The Quakers of Iowa* (Iowa City: The State Historical society of Iowa, 1914), p. 98.

9. Joel Bean, "The Issue", *The British Friend; A Monthly Journal Devoted to the Interests of the Society of Friends*, vol. XXXIX, No. III, 3rd. Month 1st., 1881, p. 49.

10. From a private letter by Stacy Bevan, one of the two Friends traveling in the ministry, as quoted by Darius B. Cook, *History of Quaker Divide (Iowa): Struggles and Accomplishments of First Settlers. The Story of their Achievement forms interesting reminiscences in the history of Early Days — Meetings, Schools, Farm and Home Life* (Dexter, Iowa: The Dexter *Sentinel*, 1914), p. 66.

11. Cook, pp. 67-70.

12. L.T. Jones, p. 103.

13. Query No. 7, *Iowa Yearly Meeting, Revised Discipline*, 1876.

14. As quoted in Cook, pp. 79-83, from the minutes of the Conference of
174

Friends held at Bear Creek, Fifth Month 29, 1877. also see L.T. Jones, pp. 165-167.

15. Cook, p. 83-85. Also see L.T. Jones, pp. 167-169.

16. *Minutes of Iowa Yearly Meeting of Friends*, 1877, p. 4

17. *Minutes of Iowa Yearly Meeting of Friends*, 1878, p. 10.

18. L.T. Jones, p. 94.

19 . Cook, p. 85.

20. Cook, p. 86.

21. As quoted by Cook, pp. 89-90, from the General Advices in Book of Discipline of Iowa Yearly Meeting (C).

22. This was written by Ella Newlin in 1945, as a post script to her account of the separation that she had written in 1935. Her account is largely a precis of that written by Cook and hence is not quoted in this chapter. I am grateful to Margaret Smith Lacey, an Iowa Conservative Friend, who presented a photocopy of Ella Newlin's typescript to me.

Chapter 14

1. Willard Heiss, *A Brief History of Western Yearly Meeting of Conservative Friends and the Separation of 1877* (Indianapolis: John Woolman press, 1963), quotes in anonymous letter in his possession to the effect that: "For several years prior to 1877 there were introduced into the Society doctrinal teachings and practices which were at variance with the accepted doctrines of the Society..." p. 3.

2. See: Elliott, p. 98.

3. *Minutes of Western Yearly Meeting*, minute 22, p. 12, 1877.

4. *Minutes of Western Yearly Meeting*, minute 66, p. 78, 1878.

5. *Minutes of Western Yearly Meeting*, minute 33, p. 32, 1879.

6. Walter Robson, *The British Friend*, October, 1913, p. 288. Willard Heiss disagrees with the number withdrawing. He reported about two hundred leaving the meeting house. See: Heiss, p. 5.

7. Robson.

8. Heiss, p. 31.

9. See: Sheldon Glenn Jackson, *A Short History of Kansas Yearly Meeting of Friends* (Wichita: Days Print Shop, 1946), p. 56.

10. Jackson, pp. 56-57.

11. *Minutes of Kansas Yearly Meeting*, minute 4, p. 2., 1879.

12. *Minutes of Kansas Yearly Meeting*, minute 15, pp. 6-7, 1879.

13. *Minutes of Cottonwood Monthly Meeting*, 12th mo. 24th., 1879.

14. *Minutes of Cottonwood Quarterly Meeting*, 1st mo. 12th., 1880.

15. *Minutes of Kansas Yearly Meeting*, minute 11, pp. 5-6, and minute 35, p. 19, 1880.

16. Jackson, p. 58-59.

17. Jackson, p. 59.

Chapter 15*

(*This chapter is a revision of a paper given to the Canadian Friends Historical Association in October, 1987. The paper appeared in the Winter, 1987, issue of the Canadian Friends Historical Newsletter.)

1. Arthur G. Dorland, *The Quakers in Canada, A History* (Toronto: The Ryerson press, 1968).

2. Pelham Monthly Meeting, minutes of 7th. month, 7th., 1875. I am here using the dates as given in the minutes and not following Dorland's page numbering as the original did not have numbered pages.

3. Pelham Monthly Meeting, minutes of 1st. month, 1st., 1879.

4. Norwich Monthly Meeting Minutes, 6th. month 14th. 1876.

6. Norwich, 11th. month 8th., 1876.

7. Norwich, 11th. month 15th., 1876.

8. Norwich, 12th. month 13th., 1876.

9. Norwich, 3rd. month 14th. 1877. and Pelham Quarterly Meeting Minutes, 2nd. month 10th., 1877.

10. Norwich, 5th, month 9th., 1877.

11. Norwich, 6 th. month 13th., 1877, and *Pelham Quarterly Meeting of Women Friends Minutes*, 6th month 16th., 1877.

12. Pelham Quarterly, 9th. month 15th., 1877.

13. Norwich, 7th. month 11th., 1877.

14. Norwich, 8th. month 8th., 1877.

15. Norwich, 9th. month 12th., 1877.

16. Norwich, 9th. month 26th., 1877.

17. Pelham Quarterly Meeting, Conservative, 9th month 15th., 1877. This meeting was renamed "Norwich Quarterly Meeting" in September, 1889 by Canada Yearly Meeting (Conservative).

18. Pelham Quarterly (C), 2nd. month. 9th, 1878.

19. Dorland, p. 237

20. Dorland, pp. 241-242.

21. Dorland, p. 242

22. Pelham Quarterly (C), 6th. Month 11th. 1881.

Chapter 16

1. An account of this is given in Allen Jay, *Autobiography of Allen Jay* (Philadelphia: The John C. Winston Co., 1910), pp. 120-125.

2. Damon, D. Hickey, "Progressive and Conservative Search for Order: The Division of North Carolina Quakers," in *The Southern Friend; Journal of the*

North Carolina Historical Society, Vol. VI, Number 1, Spring, 1984, p. 20.

3. Hickey, p. 21.

4. Hickey, p. 22.

5. Hickey, pp. 31-33.

6. These notes came from the oral family history as told by Seth Hinshaw and Algie Newlin in a personal interview conducted in Greensboro, North Carolina on May 3, 1983. This is also mentioned by D.D. Hickey, "Bearing the Cross of Plainness, A Conservative Quaker Culture in North Carolina", *M.A. Thesis*, University of North Carolina at Greensboro, 1982, p. 61.

7. Jay, chapters XV to XXV, pp. 126 to 239. Also see Hickey, thesis, p. 15.

8. See: Opal Thornburg, *Earlham:The Story of the College, 1847-1962* (Richmond, Indiana: The Earlham college Press, 1963) and Walter R. Williams, *The Rich Heritage of Quakerism*, who provide a good history of these events.

9. Jay, pp. 206-7.

10. Jay does not mention this in his autobiography. Among Friends the first person named to a committee is often the originator or proposer of the idea and as often acts as the convenor for at least the first meeting of the committee.

11. North Carolina Yearly meeting Minutes, 1870, p. 22.

12. North Carolina Yearly Meeting Minutes, 1870, p. 22.

13. The Association did not actually cease to work until 1891, see jay, pp. 222-225.

14. In spite of their opposition to the evangelicals and their contact with conservative Friends, these Friends did recognize their own weaknesses. Hickey, "Search for Order," p. 19, as quoted from Eastern Quarterly Meeting minutes of IX/24/1883.

15. North Carolina Yearly Meeting minutes, 1893, also Quoted in Hickey, thesis, p. 17.

16. See also: Hickey, "Search for order," p. 19.

17. North Carolina Yearly Meeting Minutes, 1888.

18. Hickey, thesis, p. 24.

19. See: North Carolina Yearly Meeting minutes, 1894, Minute #56, pp. 47-48.

20. Hickey, thesis, p. 26-27.

21. As quoted by Hickey, thesis, pp. 28-29, from Eastern Quarterly Meeting minute of V-28-1898.

22. Hickey, thesis, p. 31.

23. North Carolina Yearly Meeting Minutes, 1898, minute #17, p. 8.

24. North Carolina Yearly Meeting Minutes, 1900, minute #18, p. 10 also quoted in Hickey, thesis, p. 33.

25. North Carolina Yearly Meeting Minutes 1900, minute #20, p. 11, and Hickey, thesis.

26. North Carolina Yearly Meeting Minutes 1902, minute #26, p. 11.

27. The offending part of the new discipline is from ch. X, section 4. of the Uniform Discipline, and is quoted in Hickey, thesis, p. 41.

28. North Carolina Yearly Meeting Minutes, 1903, minute #17, p. 13, and Hickey, thesis, p. 40.

29. North Carolina yearly Meeting Minutes 1904, minute #30, p. 37-40, and in Hickey, thesis, pp. 42-44.

30. Hickey, thesis.

Chapter 17

(*This chapter is a revision of an article in *Quaker History*, Spring, 1988, I would here like to acknowledge the help received from the editor of that journal, Arthur J. Mekeel, with some of the problems of style I have had.)

1. From notes written by Harold Tollefson on ths separation, augmented by

an interview conducted with him by the author and Joyce Mardock Holden on June 18, 1980 in Richmond, Indiana. After his death a copy of the tape obtained during the interview was deposited in Lilly Library of Earlham College.

2. See: John J. Baldwin, "Union High School" (unpublished) and Westfield Monthly Meeting Minutes of 11th. month, 28th., 1879. Indiana's introduction of a public school system was the principal reason this took place.

3. For an account of this and other debates involving this distinguished Quaker while he was at Earlham, see Thornburg, pp. 261-272.

4. Indiana Yearly Meeting Minute No. 50, 1920.

5. Proceedings of a Joint Committee of Indiana and Western Yearly Meetings of the Society of Friends held at East Main St. Friends Church, Richmond, Indiana, beginning at 1:30 p.m., of Tuesday, Dec. 7, 1920, p. 12 (unpublished).

6. Proceedings of a Joint Committee, p. 87.

7. "Letter to Friends in Indiana Yearly Meeting", p. 9. This was printed privately and sent out generally to members of the Yearly Meeting. It is difficult to determine whether the distribution was to all members or just to those who were regarded in sympathy with the cause.

8. "An Appeal to the Membership of Indiana Yearly Meeting" and "Minority Report on Earlham College Investigation", see p. 7 and 8 of the latter. These were also printed privately.

9. Western Yearly Meeting minute 28 of 1921 and Indiana Yearly Meeting minute 54 of 1921.

10. Five Years Meeting minute 37 of 1912.

11. Indiana Yearly Meeting minutes 12 and 106 of 1921

12. *Proceedings of the Conference of Friends*, 1887, pp. 18, 65-66, 173-177, and 310.

13. Five Years Meeting Minutes of ninth month seventh, 1922 pp. 118-119. It is also quoted in Redding, pp. 20-22.

14. Earl Redding, "A Report to the General Board of Friends United Meeting concerning the History of the Affirmation of Faith and Uniform Discipline of

the Five Years Meeting of Friends," (Oskaloosa, Iowa: mimeograph), June, 1974, p. 22.

15. Redding, p. 2, as quoted from Five Years Meeting Minutes, 1922, pp. 119-120.

16. See various issues of the *Gospel Minister*, especially that of February 7, 1924, p. 1.

17. From the interview conducted with Tellofson on June 18, 1980 in Richmond, Indiana.

18. Bill, John Brent, *David B. Updegraff,* pp. 16-17.

19. Central Yearly Meeting, *1926 — Golden anniversary — 1976: History of Central Yearly Meeting of the Friends Church* (Westfield, Indiana: Central Yearly Meeting, 1976), pp. 24-39. Also see *Declaration of Faith and Discipline for Central Yearly Meeting of Friends,* adopted 1928 and amended 1960, pp. 6 and 7.

20. Central Yearly Meeting, *History*, p. 12, and Discipline, pp. 6 and 7.

21. In 1978, for example, they spent about $39,500 on their mission program, while the budget for their yearly meeting was $27,500. See: Central Yearly Meeting Minutes, pp. 13 and 25, of 1978.

Conclusion

1. Kurtz, p. 1087.

2. Kurtz, p. 1088.

3. Kurtz, p. 1089.

4. Kurtz, p. 1090.

5. See: Hans Mol, *Identity and the Sacred* (Oxford Basil Blackwood, 1976. Mol has described how peoples choices of important symbols is liked to their own self-identity and the identities they share with others. By choosing to disagree on an important issue, Friends are selecting different symbols as central to their identities and, thus, creating different identities.

INDEX

182

121-126
Number Eleven Meeting, Indiana, 138
Nuttal, Geoffrey, 15

oath(s), 12, 18, 23, 24 ,25, 34, 37, 42,
    50, 152
Ohio Yearly Meeting, 66-7, 75-6, 80-1,
    85, 89-94, 109-111, 121, 135, 137-8
Olson, Soren, 113
ordinances, 111
Oregon Yearly Meeting, 137
organs, 108
Orthodox ,49-68, 83-92, 111-133
Osborn, Charles, 79
Oskaloosa, Iowa, 116

Paxton Boys, 40
peace testimony, 1
Pearsall, Robert 105
Pelham Quarterly and Monthly
    Meeting, Ontario, 68, 121-127
Penn, William, 22, 25-31, 64
Penn, William, Sr., 25
Pennsylvania, 25-33, 40, 45, 54, 75, 80
Perrot, John , 19-23, 50
persecution, 12-22, 34, 35, 43
Philadelphia Yearly Meeting, 30, 44,
    56-8, 62, 67, 69, 70, 76, 83, 85, 86,
    89, 93, 94, 150, 151
Philadelphia elders, 54-58
pianos, 108
Pidgeon, Isaac, 113
Pickering, Ontario, 126
Pilgrim Holiness Church, 106
Plainfield, Indiana, 118
Poll Act, 24
Portland Quarterly Meeting, Ohio,
    134-142
Prairie Grove Meeting, Iowa, 112
Praemunire (See Statute of Provisors
    and Praemunire), 12
Presbyterians, 10, 12, 25, 62, 63, 80,
    99, 105, 146
Preston, Patrick, 22-31
Primitive Friends Yearly Meeting,
    Baltimore, 94-5
Progressive Friends, 80-82
Provisors (See Statute of Provisors and
    Praemunire), 12
Puritan(s), 10, 12, 25, 26, 40

Quare, Daniel, 37
queries, 36, 94, 95, 108, 115, 122-4,

152

Randolph Meeting, Indiana, 138
Ranter(s), 9, 11, 15, 29
Ravnaas, Anna, 112
Rese, Hulda, 106
Revival(s), 106, 107, 112-15, 119, 129-
    31
Rhode Island Yearly Meeting, 28, 86
Rice Jones, 13
Rich, Mary, 84
Rich Square Meeting, N. C., 128-133
Richard II, 12
Richmond Conference of Friends, 111,
    130-33, 136-37
Richmond Declaration of Faith, 110,
    130-37
Richmond, 132-33,
Robson, Elizabeth, 56, 63
Robson, Walter, 119
Rodman ,Elizabeth, 84
Russell, Elbert, 135

sacraments, 109, 110, 11
sacrilege, 1, 44, 50, 51, 55, 146, 152,
    153
Salem, Iowa, 112, 113
Salem Quarterly Meeting, Ohio, 80
salvation, 37, 70, 72, 94, 109, 111
sanctification (entire), 87, 111
Sands, David, 52, 56, 73, 146
Sargeant, John, 96-97
Saskatchewan, 98
Saskatoon, 98
saved, 111, 127
Savery, William, 52
Scattergood School, Iowa, 112
Scipio Quarterly Meeting, New York,
    68
Scott, Richenda, 99
Second Day Morning Meeting, 19, 31,
    53
Seekers, 7, 9
Shackleton, Abraham, 52
Shattered Baptists, 10
Shaw, Benjamin, 84
Shillitoe, Thomas, 56, 63, 64
Simmonds, Martha, 14
Six Weeks Meeting, 19
slave(s)(ry), 31, 41, 43, 54, 69, 75-82,
    95
Smith, Elizabeth, 123
Smith, Hanna Whitall, 105
Smith, Timothy L., 105, 106

185

186